the
CORPORATE
PRAYER
CHALLENGE

30 Days
to Kickstart
the Change
We Need

Howard Lawler

The Corporate Prayer Challenge: 30 Days to Kickstart the Change We Need

Copyright © 2020 by Howard Lawler

Salpizo Publications
Wake Forest, NC

ISBN: ISBN 978-0-578-75530-4

DEDICATION

To my wife Francine who prays well with others

CONTENTS

A CHALLENGE

Once upon a (real) time

Odd or even? Because the government cared, I had to
know the last digit on the license plate of my aqua, white-
vinyl-topped, 1963 Buick Skylark. Even a stylish ride runs
out of gas.

Perhaps you never heard of the gas shortage of the 1970s.
I lived it. Long lines at the pump plagued drivers, and the
inflated prices added insult to injury. In 1974 the United
States government divided the driving public into odd and
even to cope with the problem through gas rationing. You
could only buy fuel on even days with an even last plate
number and on odd days with an odd number. I forget how
zero counted.

Time for a change

That gas shortage is a thing of the past. This book addresses a current crisis: a corporate prayer shortage in the church. Members and attendees might not realize it, but the shortage inflicts significant damage.

Corporate prayer is the last thing many churches want to do. In many cases it is minimal. In some places, it is *not* done. That zero counts a lot.

Our prayer-deficient state is odder than a license plate ending in 3, 5, or 7. Prayer fuels church life and God places no limit on it. We have created this shortage, and we need to fix it.

It will not be easy. It will be *good* for everyone.

I approach writing on prayer with sane fear. I resonate with P. T. Forsyth who wrote, "It is a difficult and even formidable thing to write on prayer, and one fears to touch the Ark."[1] God forbid that I pose as an expert or prayer enthusiast. I dispel that notion with a confession in the first chapter.

I also fear sounding like a scold. Do you wonder if I have a superior attitude? Turn to the sixth chapter.

Prayer is an especially touchy subject as the fourth chapter shows. Even a non-scolding book on corporate prayer touches a nerve like a dentist shooting cold air into an open cavity. The dentist does well but does not make fans. The truth, like a tooth, can hurt. A Turkish proverb says to have one foot in the stirrup if you speak the truth. Writing a book like this means nailing both feet to the ground. Despite the risk, I am taking up the challenge.

My book presents the bright prospect of improved church health, yet it is more sobering than most books I have seen on prayer. I share encouraging episodes, but also lessons learned in disappointing circumstances. I do so, not as personal therapy, but rather as pastoral testimony. I am not interested in producing a best-seller; I desire to be the best teller of hard lessons learned.

I will use no names (or even give identifying hints) when I relate disturbing comments that have been made to me about prayer. It helps that I have served multiple congregations and have formed wide associations. I draw from many years in the pastorate, thereby ruining attempts to sleuth identities. I would rather have omitted those comments, but they provide practical cases and show the problem's depth.

My grandfather used to say that some people act like they were weaned on dill pickles. I am not a sour person. If you are one, feel free *not* to introduce yourself to me. This book reflects my zany life fraught with humor. I might be the only pastor to use foam, polyester batting, paint, styrene rod, half of a baboon mask, ping pong balls, a pool noodle, and an RC car to fabricate a five-foot-long, remote-controlled mouse for a children's event. If I have a twin in this mouse matter, please introduce yourself to me.

I laugh a lot, but I *cannot* laugh off our lack of prayer.

Tapping into my inner Bob Ross and producing a happy little book would please me, but I cannot do that given what I observe. The situation is serious. I am not a harsh man, but I do not use soft-soap on the Lord's sheep. I am calling for the church to repent as one who has had to repent.

I facilitated the prayer shortage as a pastor. I *grieve* that I helped produce this sad state. I intend to do what I can to change things for the better.

This book is for all church members, not just for pastors or other leaders. We all need to embrace corporate prayer. We all must be part of the solution to our problem.

I especially desire to help seminarians who will serve in a North American church context, one like it, or one influenced by it. Those preparing for such ministry need to know what they face and what is at stake. As one who has served as a pastor in this culture for almost four decades, I know.

Renowned author George Orwell explained why he wrote. "I knew that I had a facility with words and a power of facing unpleasant facts."[2] In a modest approximation of that summary, I acknowledge that the Lord has gifted me with the facility, and has disciplined me into the power.

I also dare to claim modest affinity with Helmut Thielecke. In the preface to <u>The Trouble with the Church,</u> he wrote, "For many people what is written here may be an offense. But, believe me, it was a pressing need that compelled me to speak. I could not bear any longer *not* to say what is said in the following pages." His preface also addressed his direct manner. "This is a personal word and a personal concern and distress, and I dispense with caution and any attempt to guard and qualify my statements at every point."[3]

I do not qualify my critique by noting the many good things the church is doing in America. Yet I cannot accept those good things as a reason to ignore one great, imperative thing that generally is not being done. We dare not avoid facing the void.

The Apostle Paul told the Ephesian church elders, "I did not avoid proclaiming to you anything that was profitable" (Acts 20:20). Avoidance is bad stewardship, so I avoided avoidance and wrote a book to help the church.

Paul told those same leaders, "Be on guard for yourselves and for all the flock of which the Holy Spirit has appointed you as overseers, to shepherd the church of God, which he purchased with his own blood" (Acts 20:28). Writing a book is easy compared to what Jesus did for us. Paying for sins to build the church is the hardest work anyone ever did. Writing and reading about prayer is nothing in comparison.

Will you spend a little time?

I challenge you to devote a few minutes a day to face the prayer condition of the church and begin to improve it. I do not provide formulas in this book – I platform fundamentals. My book does not promise mature corporate prayer in a month. I do not work miracles. If you work your way through my book, however, you will gain a perspective that will help you in the long run.

This book provides 30 brief chapters to fit a one-month reading approach. The average reader supposedly chomps sentences at a rate of 200 words per minute. You could chew-up a day's reading in about five to ten minutes. How long you ruminate is up to you.

My Buick was great. I miss that ride. I wanted a 1960s era Triumph motorcycle. Alas, I did not get that one. I never knew the thrill of kickstarting the classic bike and running the open road. I leaned into no curves and felt no rushing wind. Too bad. The ride would have been worth some bugs stuck in my teeth.

Are you up for a better, bug-free trip? Will you join me in exploring challenging terrain by God's sure word? Do you dare to kickstart the change we need? That outcome will provide triumph enough for me, and prove adventure enough for anyone.

PART ONE

PASSION AND PRECISION

Two goals drive this part of the book: transparency and precision. Honest confession will attain the first goal, and clear definition the second.

FIRST A CONFESSION

I start with bracing honesty. The confession might seem shocking coming from the author of a book on prayer. Brace yourself.

I don't have a passion for prayer.

There, I said it. But what do I mean by "passion?" I mean a strong natural attraction or driving emotion.

Don't misunderstand. I do *not* mean that I rarely feel like praying. I mean that feelings do not drive me to pray. It is wonderful when I keenly feel the pull, but God gave me a will to use when things are not wonderful. People tell me that my confession about passion moves them to pray. They realize they too can fight doldrums and disinclination.

Maybe you picked up this book because you *do* have a passion for prayer. I am glad if you do. Maybe I will get there in this life.

I have other passions. For example, I naturally love playing trumpet. Even though it is a hard and humbling instrument, I run to all kinds of playing sessions. I have played for over 50 years, and I feel as ready to play as ever. No one commands me to play the trumpet – I do it eagerly.

There is a big difference between a trumpet and corporate prayer, and it explains (in part) my feelings. I own a trumpet; the trumpet does not own me. The trumpet is hard to master, but facing a holy master is far more sobering. God is more than our master, of course, but he is not less.

I do not eagerly run to prayer meetings, but I go. Why? I have *an obedience* for prayer.

The living God commands me to pray as an individual and as part of his church. God does not demand that I eagerly run to prayer gatherings, but he does call me to obey by praying. I never regret having gone to prayer sessions, but I must often push myself through the door. I choose to use my will to honor the word of God. Jesus said obeying his commands is the mark of love for him (Jn 14:15).

Love, as Jesus used the word, is not a mere passion. Love is a tenacious drive to honor God, one that's grown in me since conversion. The Lord's amazing grace created and nourishes my love for him.

My dad had a passion for steam railroading. When he took me on excursions, he taught me all about motive power in engine operations. He would point to the pipe that delivered sand to the wheels to help the locomotive overcome steep grades.

My motive power for prayer is *grace*, not guilt.

Books on prayer often say that guilt is not the author's goal, and it certainly is not mine in this book. I fear, however, that we have downplayed the usefulness of guilt. If some people who read this book need to feel guilty, so be it. I need to experience guilt when I violate God's word. Good grief exists in more than Peanuts comic strips (2Cor 7:8-9).

Proper guilt helps get us back on track, but guilt does not help us make the grade to our destination. My will to pray is grit delivered by grace. Truth and mercy drive obedience and progress.

Exercise bracing honesty of your own. Do you obey God's call to pray? Do you call on his grace for the grit to make the grade in private prayer and corporate prayer? If not, why not?

I did not write this book as a noble person, so keen to pray. I did not write this book so that you would become that person, nice as the prospect may be. I wrote this book because we all need to *obey* and *pray*. If you thought you were going to read the lofty thoughts of an expert prayer practitioner, you picked up the wrong book. If you are that person, maybe you should write a book. It might help me.

Stay with the upgrade theme but shift to a mountain climbing metaphor. Corporate prayer seems like ascending Mount Everest. I do not deny the challenge, and I will not make a molehill out of this mountain. I know we can make the grade, however, because we have much better help than Himalayan Sherpas, amazing as those Everest guides are. We have the gracious, omnipotent Savior.

Ready to go for higher ground?

FIRST THINGS FIRST

know. This is the second day, so how can "First Things First" serve as the heading?

The banner does not concern the flow of the book but marks the start of definition. This is base camp for the journey. I will define the *topic* and *target*. I delineate the behavior and the audience to whom I call.

The topic

This book calls for "corporate prayer." What do I mean by those two words? We must deal with my definition of the activity before unpacking details and addressing problems.

In our culture, people commonly think of big business when they hear the word "corporate." Terms like "corporate structure," "corporate raider," "corporate downsizing," or "corporate profits" come to mind. We think of corporations like IBM, GM, or MGM. Toss aside that meaning for this book's purposes.

You might as well toss my book now if you don't mark my meaning.

I am using the word "corporate" in a biblically informed way. The word comes from the Latin term "corpus," meaning "a body." The human body has many parts but is a living whole. The body became a metaphor for a group of people functioning as one.

The church is the Christian body of believers (1Cor 12). The local church is not a business; it is a living body. We transcend mere metaphors here and encounter true mystery. We cannot grasp the full meaning of that corporate reality, but we must use what we can grasp to get a handle on the prayer life of the church.

Some people apply the label "corporate prayer" to any case where believers pray together. For example, they might apply it to the same few folks gathering in a prayer meeting each week from a church of many. Those few folks are members of the body praying together, but how corporate is their prayer experience? Another example is a portion of a church praying in small groups with the same few people in each group. That experience does not give much weight to the adjective "corporate."

We could just as easily apply the label "corporate" to *any* activity a handful of church members do. At that point, the adjective becomes weightless. We should give the word some heft or let it float off like a helium balloon.

When we lack prayer beyond affinity groups, using the term "corporate prayer" serves to camouflage our problem. Why not be real and fully embrace the adjective? Why not make ways to pray well beyond a small group in the local church?

The problem worsens when we move from neglect to rejection. When people refuse to pray beyond their affinity group, we should not apply the wrong label to mask manifest obstinacy. If people will only pray with people they choose, they do not appreciate the reason God chose to make a body of believers.

There must at least be willingness to pray with *anyone* in the body for "corporate prayer" to serve as a meaningful label.

Church members are often enthusiastic about church business meetings as a place of influence, but not enthusiastic about prayer meetings. Do we find that distressing? When we long to express our democratic voice more than talk to our Lord as his people, we have lost our way.

Shouldn't corporate prayer give people exposure to the larger body? Shouldn't we seek to pray in a way that gives rich expression to our corporate identity? Considering how few people have that rich experience, shouldn't we speak more about *corporate prayerlessness* than about corporate prayer?

The label "corporate prayer" reasonably applies to prayer shared by the larger body. Most American evangelical churches lack that experience. We can properly speak of prayer happening in those churches, but speaking about corporate prayer stretches language to the breaking point.

I applaud prayer by individuals, by couples, by families, in small groups, by ministry teams, in staff meetings, in colleges, at special breakfasts, at conferences, on retreats, at rallies, in regional prayer convocations, for national days of prayer, by the pastor from the pulpit, and more.

We need more. We need to pray as the body.

We come to the point of definition. My definition of corporate prayer is *prayer gatherings in which anyone from a local church might participate, and in which all kinds of people from that church do participate.*

The adjective "corporate" has weight when people assemble for prayer across demographic lines, age, marital status, maturity, talent, economic status, race, passions, temperament, and any other category the world uses to sort people. The adjective is hefty when participation in prayer is not exceptional but standard.

Picture a town square in past centuries. People could meet in small groups in many other places in town, but everyone met in the town square for important purposes. If only the same few people showed up, the town would not have a functioning square. It would have a concept of a square, but not a corporate reality. Similarly, the same few people meeting for prayer indicates a church does not have functional corporate prayer.

For me, corporate prayer is square prayer.

Picture a Medieval village whose Lord of the Manor was grand yet also gracious. He calls all the citizens to the town square to talk. Except for a small group, the people ignore the call or refuse to take part. That scenario plays out in churches across America every week. We disregard the most grand and gracious Lord (Col 1:1-22; 2:6-15).

Corporate prayer always happens in a group setting. But group prayer is not always corporate prayer in the full sense of the word. During corporate prayer, over time, you hear the hearts of those who will never be in your home, in your small group, or your circle of close friends. The one commonality is Jesus.

We practice a lot of divvy-up ministry. We need to *un-divvy*. Go beyond praying with your friends, spouse, family, ministry team, age group, or any other legitimate form for clustered prayer. Go back to prayer as practiced by churches before demographics became the rage and ministry silos dotted the landscape. A church that thinks as a body will pray as a body. Form and function unite here because a corpus is a united entity.

What about liturgical prayer? It unites the church in prayer, but it is not enough. The assembly in Acts 1 certainly went beyond liturgical prayer, as did the church when praying under persecution in Acts 4 and Acts 12. The body voiced all kinds of joys and concerns to the Lord.

God made no mistake when he made the body. Pray that way, and prove his wisdom is glorious. Cross into the corpus zone. It is a great place to live and pray.

The target

To whom am I making my call in this book? What church culture am I critiquing?

The audience is the American evangelical church. That phrase means *the prevailing evangelical church culture found in North America.*

My book is an inside job, speaking to the church culture in which I became a Christian, and for which I have ministered as a pastor. My concern extends to churches that are like the North American evangelical church culture, and have been significantly influenced by it. If such churches are in South America, Europe, or other places, they come into the sphere of my call.

As for evangelical churches in North America who are strong in corporate prayer, I do not call them to repent. I encourage them to remain strong.

My concern is not geography; it is practical ecclesiology. We have a lot of experience and expertise in various forms of ministry. But we are very weak in corporate prayer. Why?

The problem is not time. We make time for what we deem a priority. We have the same number of minutes in a day as did Jesus. He multiplied loaves and fish, but he did not multiply minutes and hours. He did not do a miracle to make more time; he simply made time to pray. The Son did not stop the sun in the sky; he stopped to pray alone and with others. He made prayer a priority.

The problem is not logistics. We can devise various

ways to promote corporate prayer. We do it all the time for other concerns.

Shine the light on the real culprits: *desire* and *determination.*

The second one is vital. Determination to do the right thing can overcome the desire to do nothing. Determination is indispensable because it is scary to disrupt the status quo. I am convinced it is the best thing we can do.

We will pay a price, and we will make mistakes – that much is obvious. But we must not use the obvious to obscure sad facts. We show a tepid desire for prayer and little determination. The American evangelical church has not tried hard enough to pray together as the body.

Try hard. It is high time we did.

PART TWO

PRAYER AND PROBLEMS

We must face real problems if the American evangelical church will pray as God requires. With his help, we can triumph. Keep the bright prospect of grace-based progress in mind as you read the sobering parts in this section.

A RARE ONE FOR THE BOOKS

"There is no end to the making of many books." Anyone with access to a search engine can prove that Ecclesiastes 12:12 is accurate. The same proof applies to books about prayer. Unlike gasoline in 1974, no shortage exists.

I have been on a quest, searching my bookshelves, bookstores, libraries, and the Internet for books dedicated to corporate prayer. Keep my definition in mind as you process my pursuit. I look for books about prayer gatherings in which anyone from a local body of believers might participate and in which all kinds of people from that church do.

I have found that few books mention corporate prayer. Those that do address the topic sometimes work with a different conception, and do not fulfill my quest.

Use a safari metaphor. The genus "books about prayer" is easy to spot in the field, but the species "books about corporate prayer" is not. Trek the savanna yourself. You will be surprised at what you do *not* find. When a zoologist spots a scarce specimen, it becomes "one for the books."

One sad word sums up my search: *rare*.

I happily note an uptick in such books in the last decade. But we still have a way to go to give the important practice the attention it deserves.

The paucity of publication about corporate prayer gives the impression that our main weakness is private prayer. The abundance of books on personal prayer silently suggests congregational prayer is strong. The silence keeps us from hearing the disconnect between the Bible and the prayer practices of the local church body. We mourn the time lost from private prayer, picturing Jesus waiting to meet us at devotion time. You might have seen the trope with two chairs – Jesus waits patiently in his chair, and one chair sits empty. We need a new corporate trope with Jesus facing many empty seats.

What are we waiting for?

I am grateful for the variety of authors and approaches to prayer in general, but we need more books about corporate prayer. There has barely been a beginning to the making of those books.

I realize people use other formats to address prayer. I leave it to others to assess journal articles, blogs, vlogs, tweets, and podcasts about corporate prayer. Books are still powerful media, so that is where I will focus.

The books I have found dedicated to prayer in the local church mostly address prayer happening inside the divvy-up church model. As for other books, I barely find chapters on praying as the body. We especially need books that do careful, detailed exegesis of passages about corporate prayer and apply the results to pastoral theology.

A growing number of solid books critique the American evangelical church and address vital issues like sound doctrine, preaching, the means of grace, church discipline, authority, and holiness. Even those books rarely mention corporate prayer. In evangelical publishing, it is a great omission.

General ministry books call the evangelical church to pursue church health and growth in various ways. For example, it is supposedly imperative to provide a clear path to discipleship. That phrase usually means we must create a programmatic, sequential approach for developing devoted followers of Christ. But the clear path to *making disciples* is already in the Bible: repent, believe, and be baptized. After that, already-made-disciples grow through obedience in every area of life. The Great Commission says so (Matt 28:19-20).

The gospel applied in salvation makes disciples. Those disciples decide to pray as directed or not. To decide not to do so compromises mission and undermines maturity. All-embracing obedience includes corporate prayer. To neglect that part is a clear path to fruitlessness.

We are in trouble when we designate as imperative what is not in the New Testament, yet regard as optional what it models for us. There is no delineated, sequential maturity process in the New Testament. There is corporate prayer throughout the New Testament. That scriptural discipline is almost invisible in our books.

Evangelicals need more books devoted entirely to corporate prayer, but we need even more than that. Prayer by the body should enjoy greater representation in books about prayer in general, in theology books, in books that analyze ministry philosophy and strategy, and in books that examine the church and culture.

The Book of Acts shows the church praying as a congregation. Prayer fueled the early church to pursue the great commission. Why don't we find more books (or at least whole chapters) addressing that vital practice today?

Consider one factor that flies under the radar: *local church life profoundly influences evangelical academics.* The local church *forms books* as much as *books inform* the local church.

The practice of cross-body prayer is rare in our church pews and padded chairs, so related publication is rare. Congregational experience shapes commentaries and other materials by scholars. Pastors lead congregations. So, pastors influence academics more than we think we do.

Local church shepherds are crucial to the change we need regarding prayer by the body. Pastors must drive corporate prayer. Nothing less will do.

Along with other church leaders, pastors must reshape ministry to reflect the biblical priority of corporate prayer. We need determination to fill the void, even if we must drag our desires behind us for a while to do so. We must shape future commentators and curriculum writers by corporate prayer in the church. The books will reflect the improvement in the body and reinforce it.

My dad sometimes told a joke about a lighthouse keeper. The keeper always slept through the harbor horn blasts because he grew accustomed to the noise. One night, however, the horn failed to sound. The keeper jumped up from his bed and yelled, "What was that I didn't hear?"

We need to wake up and notice the deafening silence. We should hear much more about the prayer life of the church as the body. Please receive my book as one small horn.

In 1907, E. M. Bounds trumpeted a warning about church prayer. "It is out of date, almost a lost art, and the greatest benefactor this age could have is the man who will bring the preachers and the Church back to prayer.[1] I do not presume to be that man. Perhaps no one needs to be that person.

A lot of little horns could do the job.

THE LAST THING THE PASTORS WANTED TO TALK ABOUT

They are all good guys, good pastors, and my friends. Nonetheless, they clobbered me. They did not plan the attack. No one saw it coming, but no one missed it when it did.

We had met many times. Conversations were always cordial even when we dealt with touchy subjects. We never felt tension...until that day.

The exchange had been positive and productive as we talked about preaching. One pastor asked how much time we spent preparing sermons. Various colleagues cited hours per sermon in a typical week. Going with the flow, I asked an innocent question: how much time did we spend in prayer compared to working on sermons?

The barrage began immediately and came from some of the most experienced pastors. They accused me of pride. I replied that I simply asked a related question, but they balked. One flatly said I implied personal superiority. Then I balked and said that was the last thing I meant to communicate. Then he pitched in with the assertion that I meant to imply it. Much of the bench and bullpen flung accusations of legalism and hubris at me.

Ouch!

I came in as a fellow pastor, but somehow got traded to the Pharisee team. They were so convinced of my motives that I started to wonder about myself. Then it happened. I will never forget it – an ace reliever took the mound.

A respected, seasoned pastor said he was troubled by the reaction to my question. He told the group, "This brother is bringing up one of the most substantial issues we have ever discussed." That pitch reset the atmosphere, much to my relief.

After our meeting, a few of us went to a restaurant. One said that I had touched raw nerves (his axons and dendrites included) in that session. He also said it was good that I did it.

When good pastors are touchy about prayer, we should all call time out and take stock. Coaches cannot afford to give a bad sign. Why was it OK to ask how much time we spent working on sermons, but not how much time we spent praying? Frankly, because pastors (including yours truly) do a much better job studying and writing than we do praying. We all need to step up our game.

I will always be grateful to the pastor who spoke up in favor of prayer as a vital topic. He later made me laugh about the whole brouhaha. As the King James Version says in Proverbs 17:22, "A merry heart doeth good like a medicine." Thanks for the balm, brother!

I am grateful for another thing. At least I did not ask how much we pastors promoted corporate prayer in the body. I might have been placed in a body bag. Of course, now I am making merry. Mostly.

THE LAST THING CHURCH FOLKS WANT TO DO

have been a church member for 49 years and a pastor for 38 years. I have served five churches in three states as Senior Pastor, Associate Pastor, or Interim Pastor. Many pastoral experiences inform my perspective: serving as a denominational board member, consulting, attending conferences, leading seminars, reading widely, and forming friendships with many pastors.

Every pastor knows that it is easier to lead church members to do some things than others. I have found that *the hardest* thing of all is getting the church to take part in corporate prayer meetings. People step up to all kinds of opportunities and challenges. Corporate prayer seems to be the last thing church members want to do.

A given person might not attend a given prayer meeting for various legitimate reasons. But there are precious few good reasons why most people in a congregation cannot make it to even a few corporate prayer sessions in a quarter. From all I have seen and heard, most congregations do not achieve that modest quota.

Church-going evangelicals do not accidentally fail to show up for corporate prayer sessions. We *intend* not to show up. We actively avoid a prime venue for worship and service. The difference between congregational talk and real-world behavior forced that conclusion upon me. People have often told me they "would come to prayer meeting if it was…." I have reshaped prayer meetings in countless ways in response, but participation never substantially changed. My contacts with many pastors indicate that this resistance is tragically typical in American evangelical culture.

In many other places today (and in other periods) corporate prayer is normal.[1] North American church culture does not embrace that norm. People do not flock to prayer meetings.

Churches here talk a lot about vision. Consultants often define vision as a picture of the preferred future. Who is doing the preferring? Church vision statements abound, but none that I have seen prize corporate prayer. God does not *prefer* corporate prayer. His perfect book *requires* corporate prayer, whatever our preferences may be.

Why do contemporary American Christians avoid prayer meetings? Because the meetings make us feel weak and vulnerable. I offer this perspective as a seasoned pastor and as a fellow sinner.

Whatever a preferred future might look like in a vision

statement, our preferred present is to feel empowered. The root problem reaches back to the deep past. Adam and Eve wanted to control their own lives. We also long to be in control. Corporate prayer produces the opposite effect. The flesh feels bad, so we steer clear. We feel weak and vulnerable in prayer. We veer away, thereby making ourselves weaker and more vulnerable to our spiritual enemies (Eph 6:10-20).

What terrible irony!

Being weak and vulnerable is no reason to avoid prayer. It is a *basis for* prayer. If we were naturally strong and invincible, we would not need to ask for our daily bread, or to pray, "deliver us from the evil one" (Matt 6:13).

Many church meetings are inside our comfort zone even if they have challenging elements. Perhaps we like doing a ministry where we fill our senses with activity. Perhaps we run to a Sunday School class because we feel empowered by learning new doctrine. Perhaps we eagerly anticipate our small group meeting because we are with people we like, or who are like us. Perhaps we enjoy going to a church concert, film, breakfast, tea, sports league, or rally.

But corporate prayer is last on our "I can't wait to get to that meeting!" list.

Grab an average Sunday bulletin and note how many experiences a church offers each week. Now look for corporate prayer. Is it there? If not, why not? If so, how many people seize the opportunity?

When we like doing something, or we think it is vital, we find a way to do it despite challenges and obstacles. If not, we make excuses even if the thing is not hard to do. We pave the path of avoidance with rationalizations. I have heard them as a church member. I have enabled them as a pastor. I have used them as a sinner. The same obstacles disappear when we see a movie, visit a friend, take a class, pursue a hobby, or attend a party.

Senior citizens have told me they did not come to our weeknight prayer meetings because they would not go out at night. They also did not come to the Sunday prayer meetings, which were offered at a reasonable time in the morning. Some of the seniors who made that comment came out week after week, at night, in the dead of winter, to rehearse with the special Christmas choir. Their pitch is off.

How many times have you spent a full hour at a church concert? How many times have you spent a full hour socializing with church friends? How many times have you spent a full hour in a class studying the Bible? How many times have you spent a full hour in a church committee meeting?

Now, how many times have you spent a full hour in corporate prayer? If you have, when was the last time?

People resist concentrated corporate prayer. They do not mind a small portion of a meeting (small group, Sunday School class, committee meeting) spent in prayer. A dedicated prayer meeting is all about prayer. That seems too much to bear.

Sunday services raise the stakes. Why not devote 15 full minutes of each Sunday service to corporate prayer? We know. Every disinclined person would have to endure discomfort regularly, or become Houdini and escape in public.

We regularly and happily spend sizeable chunks of time doing things with the church family. The list is long. Prayer is the outlier. Corporate prayer is time zones away.

We find corporate prayer hard to take. We hit the road. Sinclair Ferguson refers to Jonah trying to run from God's plan and aligns the fleeing prophet with our prayerlessness. "Prayer has become the hardest thing in the world for us to do. Poor Jonah! Poor evangelicalism! Yet there is a way back. There is the sign of Jonah – the cross."[2]

E. M. Bounds wrote, "Praying is spiritual work; and human nature does not like taxing, spiritual work. Human nature wants to sail to heaven under a favoring breeze, a full, smooth sea. Prayer is humbling work. It abases intellect and pride, crucifies vainglory, and signs our spiritual bankruptcy, and all these are hard for flesh and blood to bear."[3]

Take heart. Jesus has a perfect human nature, and he blazed the trail of sanctifying humility before us. See how well that turned out and follow.

Corporate prayer makes us uncomfortable. So what? Soldiers are not supposed to be comfortable all the time. In 2Timothy 2:3-4, Paul wrote, "Share in suffering as a good soldier of Christ Jesus. No one serving as a soldier gets entangled in the concerns of civilian life; he seeks to please the commanding officer." Do not avoid. Advance! God will like it. Maybe in time we too will learn to like corporate prayer.

Even if we do not learn it in time, by God's grace we have eternity.

THE LAST THING I INTENDED

"Hers was simply not a pew-shaped spine."[1] Ray Bradbury could have been describing me in that line from his story titled "Powerhouse." An Easter or Christmas Eve visit to church was nice, but (in the vernacular of the 1970s) church was "not my thing."

When people told me the gospel, I shied away. An evangelical classmate cornered me in high school gym class one day, properly concerned for my soul. Climbing the dreaded ropes appealed to me more than the eternal lifeline he tried to toss me.

I did not want to become a Christian.

The Lord had other plans. He later opened my eyes to the miracle of gospel grace. I turned to Jesus for rescue from sin and death. The best gift of all is eternal life, and receiving that gift changed my life.

Not only did God adjust my spine to fit a pew, but he also made me a pastor. William Cowper's words were proven true. "God moves in a mysterious way, his wonders to perform."[2]

The church in which I was converted was big and busy. Programs abounded. I appreciate the ways the church helped me grow, but the format shaped my idea of church in ways that did not help me grasp the proper place of corporate prayer.

Later, I became the senior pastor of an even bigger church of the same type. When a church staff gets conflicting requests to use the gym at 2:00 *am* (not 2:00 *pm*), you have a hopping church. Ours got that very request. We joked that the church needed a new name: Our Church of Perpetual Motion. We gave people what they liked, and we enjoyed substantial growth in attendance.

I have been a pastor for almost four decades and have led three program-driven churches of various sizes. I have created programs, approved programs, managed programs, staffed programs, pitched programs, expanded programs, kept some on life support, let others die, and replaced programs with new programs.

I am now convinced my former approach is the *wrong* approach.

God wants the local church to be an upward-looking, self-denying, and others-serving body. It has often become a store (small, medium, or large) providing services to individuals. I spent three decades helping it be that way. I saw measurable success at times, but I failed the whole time by marginalizing prayer. I fomented a tornado of activities that flung corporate prayer to the periphery.

I have repented.

I am not scolding anyone. I am holding myself up as a cautionary tale. Good intentions are not enough.

Perhaps you think the word "repent" should be reserved for wildly disobedient actions. Not true. We must repent whenever we leave God's prescribed path with wild abandon, or in a well-intentioned manner. Repenting means making a turn back to the right path. We get back on track driving cars even if we do not willingly choose the wrong road.

I have turned from the program-driven path. Surely, not all church programs are wrong. We should meet some felt needs. But we should not approach ministry in ways that keeps the church from being a healthy, self-giving, united, and upward-focused body. Churches cannot be fully healthy without vibrant corporate prayer. I have not forsaken all programs; I have taken corrective measures.

Prayer is now a top priority.

I cannot approach ministry the same way anymore. I cannot turn away from a conscience convinced by Scripture. I cannot repent of proper repentance.

I meant well using the attractional and programmatic church model, but I allowed prayer to be marginalized by programs. I treated prayer like a program. People saw the prayer meeting as a program for the folks who were into that kind of thing. We did not have singing meetings, sermon meetings, or communion meetings for people into those things. We did those together. Prayer meetings were like other programs, only less attractive. Many more members came to our Christian aerobics class each week than to prayer meeting!

The church needs a new approach to fitness. We have overworked our legs while running programs, but we have neglected our core. We look strong but have become flabby where it counts most. To match God's fitness standard, a ministry must be God-centered, eternity-minded, maturity-oriented, word-driven, and prayer-fueled. Ministry planning must not be about what any of us wants, including the senior pastor. It must be about what God wants and deserves.

We need corporate prayer as more than a periodic pursuit or a recourse for emergencies. The American church needs to stop its tense, frantic, shallow approach to ministry. We must make a holy turn.

God wants a holy church, not a popular one. In God's eyes, bigger is not better. God knows that better is bigger. Real growth means becoming more holy. Holy is not a size; holy is a state of being. My son is six-foot-two. When he was born, I did not set that height as a goal. I pursued his health. His size was the effect, not the objective. Health produced the right growth for his body. Health is also the right goal for churches.

I never intended to harm the church. I did harm it, however, by marginalizing prayer through programming and by positioning prayer as a program. Too bad I did not concentrate on church health. *My bad.*

I am not beating myself up; I am facing up to the facts. Pummeling oneself accomplishes nothing; pointing to lessons learned profits many. Please profit from my mistake. Make prayer with the body a top priority.

TWO PROBLEMS

Many years ago, our church van was in a repair shop. As I waited in the garage office, I saw a portrait of Jesus on the wall. He was speaking words that are not from the Bible but are true. The painting represented him telling us, "I never said it would be easy, but it will be worth it."

It won't be easy shifting to corporate prayer in our churches, but it *will* be worth it.

Mechanics look under a car hood and say, "There's your problem." I have no clue about engine repairs, but I have learned much by doing ministry. Allow me to point out two cultural problems we American evangelicals must overcome to move forward.

Individualism

There is nothing wrong with being an individual. Some of my best friends are individuals.

I am all for individuality. I can prove it with a graph. Many senior pastors took part in a survey about self-care practices. When the degree candidate published the results of his study, I detected myself on a graph for the only time in my life. The bar graphs for "plays golf," "plays tennis," and "jogs" loomed like a skyline. A thin line was barely visible amid those tall towers. Only one pastor answered, "plays roller hockey." Me. Yet, with all my individuality, I can't play hockey apart from a team. There is (if you skip-read the letters in reverse) a "me" in "team," but "we" is the way churches win.

I am all for individual liberty for citizens of the United States. A collectivist government is a nightmare. My trips to Romania after Nicolae Ceaușescu's dictatorship passed proved it. I stood on the street with an aged man who told me how the dictator's thugs knocked on his door and said the family had one hour to remove what they could carry. The thugs bulldozed his house to fulfill grand government plans. His life was never the same. He offered to sell us a tomato to help him get by. Such are the fruits of communism.

Free association and private property rights accomplish more than a statist approach. The state is not God. The real God does not offer us dreams of collectivist utopia; he creates a church in which individual Christian liberty has a wide range. His prime concern, though, is building the body. God's real-world plan for Christian community beats fantasy utopias hands down.

Being an individual is fine. The "ism" is the problem. Individualism is a worldview that gives prime place to personal independence and satisfaction.

American culture hosts a virulent strain of individualism. I say that despite deep appreciation for our freedoms and accomplishments. I recognize that Americans band together well in a crisis, are charitable, and are quite sociable. Many citizens have made profound sacrifices for our country. Yet, all that acknowledged, we prize our individual rights, likes, dislikes and choices. That independent spirit helped the pioneer farmers bust sod in the old West, but rugged individualism is poor soil in which to plant a church as a cohesive fellowship. Pampered individualism is the worst.

God loves the individual believer, yet God is no fan of individualism. God's community prizes Christ. Individuals become believers, but individualism clashes with Christianity. It prevents believers from experiencing church life as God intends.

Individualism is a body snatcher.

How can you detect if American individualism is getting in the way of your Christian life? Watch out if you always read the word "you" as singular in the Bible. That is one warning sign. Test yourself now. Philippians 4:6 says, "Don't worry about anything, but in everything, through prayer and petition with thanksgiving, present your requests to God." How does the word "your" in that verse strike you?

Do you hear a message primarily for a church, or to an individual? Paul wrote to a church.

The Lord often warms my heart personally when I read his word. That is wonderful. But my reading is warped if I can no longer see the plurals indicated by context. You do not need to know Greek to spot the communal element. A peek at the context will do. Individualism forms a bad lens for reading Scripture because it filters out many valuable lessons, including those about corporate prayer. Scriptural context often points to communal prayer.

We will never solve our problem with corporate *prayer* until we improve our quality of corporate *life*.

Daniel Henderson and Margaret Saylar clarify the issue by going back to Acts. "The believers in Acts experienced a balanced diet of corporate spirituality as they engaged in 'the apostles teaching and to [sic] the fellowship and to the breaking of bread and to prayer' (Acts 2:42). Obviously, prayer was one of the vital components of their corporate experience and personal learning. We need to create a new sense of community in prayer to help people rise above their individualistic bent."[1]

In 1944, Daniel Jenkins exposed the root of the problem. "The chief reason for the poverty of the prayer life in our midst today is not our intellectual difficulties about the reality of prayer but the miserable poverty of our common life together in the Body of Christ on earth."[2] His comment maintains relevance as I write 75 years later.

Consumerism

Here again, the "ism" is the problem because the viewpoint places a premium on consumption. People have always consumed goods and services, but consumerism is a relatively new worldview.

I believe that a free market economy works well for the United States. It harnesses self-interest better than other economic systems. It helps more people than other approaches do, even when it does so by unintended consequences. It works for me. I can try garage B, C, D, and E if I dislike how garage A services my car.

The church is different. It cannot succeed by harnessing self-interest. The gospel, when applied properly, kills self-interest. In the consumer model, churches compete for numbers. They try to determine what people want, or think they need, and then create tailored programs. Few Americans shop for churches based on a desire for corporate prayer. Prayer meeting is the Edsel (a failed Ford car – Google it) of church programs. Businesses can't market what no one wants, but believers can obey God's call to prayer as the body.

The church body as described in 1Corinthians 12-13 does not compel consumers to buy. Consumer marketing is based on self-interest, but love is not self-seeking. Love makes sacrifices. Jesus is the model.

Trevin Wax calls us to discern the danger.

In a consumerist society, worship becomes a means to an end (increasing satisfaction, albeit of the religious sense), and individualism hinders the church's ability to be a corporate witness to the gospel. We inhabit this cultural world, and, unless we are called to a society or culture in which this kind of commoditization is less present or less prominent, we will continue to live in a consumer culture. Still, Christians are not required to embrace a consumer worldview. Yes, we are consumers. We eat, make purchases, enjoy entertainments, dress ourselves, and join the common activity of a consumer culture, but living in a consumer culture and adopting a consumerist outlook on life are two different things, and we must be careful to discern the difference.[3]

Being a consumer is fine when you shop for Coca Cola, but not when you claim the cross as your life or, more properly, when Christ claims you. Corporate prayer is common where consumerism has not prevailed. It must become common in American churches.

I hasten to add that I learn from business practices. I do not spurn the source. I read the Harvard Business Review and own plenty of books on leadership from the "corporate" world. Yet, I can only mine so much ore from that vein and must process it carefully for ministry use. Gospel ministry is not a seller's market.

In addition to the prime theological problem, church marketing has a practical problem. We can see the magnitude of the predicament in <u>The Clustered World</u> by Michael Weiss. Nicknamed the "demographic detective," he has studied the science of geodemographics, which concerns marketing niches the largest companies use. Weiss notes that one company breaks America into 62 market "tribes" with names like "Scrub Pine Flats," "Shotguns and Pickups," "Towns and Gowns," "Old Yankee Rows," "Bohemian Mix," and "Money and Brains." The group "Kids & Cul-de-sacs" stands as the largest, but encompasses just 3.5 percent of the American population.[4] Weiss suggests that our nation's motto should now be "E pluribus pluriba" – "Out of many, many."[5]

How can any church customize its products to reach such a fractured society? How can any church build a diverse body by marketing to one or a few clusters? How can any church reach even most clusters?

No church can.

Marketing started to serve as a dominant ministry model about the time I was waiting on long gas lines in my Buick Skylark. It is time for the model to fade. The church does not market *a product* called the gospel. The church is *the product* of the gospel. Believers receive many benefits from the gospel, but the main point is people giving God the honor and love he deserves. The church must do that even if some people, including some church members, do not want to pay the price of discipleship.

God wants us to pray as the body. How seriously do we take his desire? Do we accept the living deity as the prime demographic? Are we devoted to pleasing him? Zach Schlegel writes, "We must push against the toxic effects of a privatized Christianity because we understand what it means to pray together as a church. In doing so, we find a God not whom we've domesticated, but who makes us tremble in awe and pray the more because he both commands us to pray and is graciously willing to hear."[6]

Cars and vans present a problem when they don't work. For church life, they can be a problem when they do. The advent of the driving public, helpful as it is, has made it hard to be the church body. Anyone who does not like church A can move on to church B, C, D, and E. I am not talking about driving past gospel-deficient churches. Discernment is different from church shopping. I am talking about professing believers shopping for the most attractive goods and services.

I do not even advocate shopping for a church by looking for corporate prayer. I am not talking about shopping at all. I am encouraging people to look for churches willing to grow in corporate prayer. I would rather drive past a church already strong in corporate prayer to join one that is seeking to grow in corporate prayer. Or walk to one for the same reason. That is not a case of church shopping; it is strategic stewardship.

A young woman in her early twenties came to our church but did not know Christ as Savior. A friend brought her to prayer meetings open to the whole church. The way the body loved and prayed for one another there deeply impressed her. She trusted Jesus for salvation. The praying of the fellowship drew her into the fellowship. Gospel-driven corporate prayer is potent.

If a pastor urges corporate prayer, some people will hit the road looking for more attractive offerings. The first gospel believers devoted themselves to prayer as the group formed by the gospel. They loved well and carried the gospel across the world. It was not easy.

It was worth it.

THE THINGS PEOPLE SAY

Perhaps the bravest parents in history were those who put their children on Art Linkletter's TV show (another opportunity to Google something). Maybe they were just reckless. The host, a kind but clever man, coaxed kids to say things that would mortify any prudent parent. The audience saw the scary spectacle of children speaking freely, off-script, under the sway of a man seeking laughs and ratings.

During my pastoral ministry some statements rate as indelible memories. I was not clever enough to see the comments coming at me, and I would not have coaxed them forward if I could. The following are real comments from nice church folks.

"I don't spend much time in prayer because I live in an attitude of prayer."

Jesus certainly lived in an attitude of prayer. But the Lord did not neglect concentrated time in prayer both alone and with others. No one ever lived with such attention to heaven as Jesus did. To use the above line about an attitude of prayer is to "cop a 'tude" about prayer. It is sassy, evasive, and verges on smugness. If we have a good attitude, we will not voice excuses for avoiding private or corporate prayer times.

"Aren't you being legalistic?"

This comment tries to ward off a pastoral call to prayer by summoning the dread specter of legalism. It implies that a pastor cannot call people to corporate prayer unless he can produce a verse that explicitly says, "Thou shalt go to prayer meeting." People who use this line ask a pastor to *be* a legalist. They want a rule.

The same people would not tell a pastor, "I will not believe in the Trinity unless you point to a verse that says, 'Thou shalt believe in the Trinity.'" The Trinity is a big picture truth evident throughout the New Testament. Corporate prayer is also evident throughout the New Testament.

Those who tell a leader they do not have to go to corporate prayer often make other pursuits mandatory. Some of those must-do things are novel, short-lived trends. Perish the thought that pastors neglect painting a picture of the preferred future, or fail to devour the latest book on post-modernism (or post-post-modernism) and the church.

Nonsense.

It *is* legalistic to tell a pastor he must do things that are not found in the Bible. It is *not* legalistic for a pastor to tell a congregation that they must come together to pray. The Bible teaches corporate prayer, not as a mere law, but as part of a new life.

Legalism is anti-gospel. Corporate prayer is a great *result* of the gospel.

Consider what Charles Spurgeon said in a Sunday sermon at the Metropolitan Tabernacle.

> It is as sure evidence of the presence of God that men pray as the rising of the thermometer is an evidence of the increase of the temperature. As the Nilometer measures the rising of the water in the Nile, and so foretells the amount of harvest in Egypt; so is the prayer-meeting a grace-ometer, and from it we may judge of the amount of divine working among a people. If God be near a church it must pray; and if he be not there, one of the first tokens of his absence will be slothfulness in prayer.[1]

The esteemed pastor knew prayer by the body was evidence of the gospel at work.

"I pray alone or with a few friends."

Great. Do more of it. But do not use that practice as a get-out-of-corporate-prayer card.

People with debilitating injuries, on military deployment, or stranded on a deserted island might have to settle for solo or small group prayer. All people will miss some prayer meetings. Car breakdowns, cold viruses, bad weather, emergencies, work schedules, and vacations result in some part of the body not being present at a given meeting.

People who *can* join the body in prayer and *refuse* to do so are another matter. John Calvin is on target saying, "we must consider that whoever refused to pray in the holy assembly of the godly knows not what it is to pray individually, or in a secret spot, or at home."[2]

Take to heart the poetry of George Herbert.

Though private prayer might be a brilliant design,
Yet public prayer has more promises, more love;
And love's a weight to hearts, to eyes a sign.
We all are but cold suitors; let us move
Where it is warmest. Leave thy six and seven.
Pray with the most; for where most pray, there is
heaven.[3]

He makes a beautiful, positive call to pray as the body. Will you take his call?

"I am not comfortable at prayer meeting."

I play music in ensembles that are above my skill level. I do not feel comfortable doing that, but I grow most in those settings. I become aware of greater musical depth and riches. The same is true of corporate prayer.

It is easier, of course, to spot musical skill levels than prayer quality. The Pharisee at the temple in Luke 18 thanked God he was not like the tax collector nearby, and he probably made his prayer sound smooth. The tax collector who repented probably sounded crude, but his prayer connected with heaven.

I have learned most from prayers that flow from humble hearts. I don't hold smooth prayers against anyone, nor should you. If that Pharisee produced a flowing prayer of repentance, it would have reached heaven. Humble hearts can connect with nimble tongues. Either way, hearts count most.

Never think that good prayers must be flowing or flowery. God loves stinky prayers if they are true prayers. I don't talk to my family in flowery verse, and I don't do so praying with God's family. Sometimes my prayers flow like molasses going uphill in January. If more people prayed when things were not flowing, fewer people would worry about praying.

"Prayer meeting is not convenient for me."

I have been in many convenience stores. One of my playful ideas is to start an inconvenience store. Everything will sit on the top shelf!

In the real world, I have never planned any prayer sessions to be inconvenient. I have done all I reasonably can do to take the opposite tack. I try to keep our busy culture in mind and to give people options. Yet, people still used the convenience line.

One person who never went to prayer meetings made the inconvenience comment even though one of our weekly prayer meetings was at the same time as our adult Sunday School classes. He attended many classes. Somehow a meeting mere steps away, at the same time, was not convenient. It is a miracle the smoke detector did not sound after his statement.

What does convenience have to do with practicing Christianity? Convenience is overrated. The church's faith is rooted in a hill called The Skull. Christianity emerged from a cross and a grave, not from a convenience store.

"You cannot force people to pray."

I don't know if I can – I never tried. I never made anyone pray out loud. I have, however, pressed church people about prayer in the church. That is not force; it is pastoral faithfulness.

This comment is an acid that dissolves any attempt to improve church behavior. It likewise destroys calls to evangelize and disciple people. Leaders need the antacid of the word to nullify this caustic excuse.

"We tried corporate prayer. It is time to try something else."

An elder made this sad and shocking comment. Prayer is not something you leave behind. Many forms of ministry are optional. Feel free to shut down a church aerobics class if people are not interested. Corporate prayer is how the body breathes. To give up on corporate prayer is deadly defeatism.

G. K. Chesterton wrote, "The Christian ideal has not been tried and found wanting; it has been found difficult and left untried."[4] The same can be said of corporate prayer in the local church. What people consider "trying it" often falls far short of true effort. Nothing can replace it.

"The change the church needs must be a work of the Holy Spirit."

In 1859, the revival in Northern Ireland surprised the church. Rev. John Mecredy served as a pastor near Belfast and wrote, "As to prayer meetings, people now delight in coming to them who could not be induced to do so before. In fact, so little interest was taken in the weekly prayer-meeting for some time previous to the outpouring of the Holy Spirit upon our people, that it was about to be given up."[5] The Holy Spirit saved the pastor from making a big mistake.

The change the church needs must be a work of the Holy Spirit. Agreed. But that fact does not absolve pastors from pressing the issue. The Bible is the work of the Holy Spirit. The Holy Spirit works to make receptive pastors and parishioners alike proactive about the word of God. The Bible tells the church to pray.

Prayer has often produced revival, and revival has often produced prayer. But prayer transcends periodic revivals. The Holy Spirit wrote Acts 2:42 which shows regular prayer is to be a *consistent practice* of the church. We need not look for extraordinary moments. We just need to maintain momentum in normal corporate prayer.

"Pastor, why aren't you sponsoring a trip to the regional prayer event?"

That comment came, with some agitation, from someone who rarely went to one of our two weekly prayer meetings. I explained, without agitation, that starting at home base is a matter of integrity. We could drive to a big event after we walked the talk as a local church. Big events bring excitement, but regular prayer in the local church best promotes health.

"You make us feel like bad Christians"

I will use a classic counselor's response to that comment. "I don't make you feel anything. You choose to feel something in response to me. Is your response a good one or not?"

In 2Corinthians 13:5 Paul told the Corinthian church, "Test yourselves to see if you are in the faith. Examine yourselves. Or do you yourselves not recognize that Jesus Christ is in you? – unless you fail the test." That must have stung, but he was not abusive. He encouraged them in the same context.

Our culture puts a premium on feeling good. Paul did not. The church must follow God's word, not feelings. The Bible shows the body praying and tells the church to pray. Feeling bad is, at best, a prod. Do what is good.

The bottom line

The preceding prayer-evading statements prove that we have a problem. They all translate to the following: "We don't like corporate prayer. We don't appreciate a pastor telling us that we must take part."

Sorry. Just doing my job.

My mom and dad did their job. They prudently kept me off the Art Linkletter show. Kids saying wild things can be entertaining; believers doing so is disturbing. We must stop saying wild things to dodge corporate prayer. It is time to grow up. In 1Corinthians 13:11 Paul said, "When I was a child, I spoke like a child, I thought like a child, I reasoned like a child. When I became a man, I put aside childish things."

What do we say to that?

THINGS THAT TEMPORARILY SHUT MY MOUTH

At times, even with my Irish gift of gab, I find myself speechless. For example, a professing believer came to my office for counseling. We talked about feeding on God's word, and she said, "I have read the Bible once. Why would I read it again?" She reduced the Bible to the level of a mediocre novel.

Another gob-smacking encounter happened in the coffee shop of a renowned Christian college. I told a student I was working on a project about the Apostle Paul. She said, "I have read his stuff – but I don't care for it." She reduced an apostle to the level of a third-rate novelist.

My rare speechless episodes pass quickly. I caught my breath and said redemptive things to both of those people. Perhaps the comments I said to them will wend their way into another book. For this book, I will relate another breathtaking statement, and what I said after the pause passed.

A pastor said that I had elevated corporate prayer to the level of the gospel. He did that to nullify my emphasis on corporate prayer.

The first two comments above came from immature sheep. The third one is a serious accusation leveled at a shepherd by a shepherd. Putting anything in the same place as the gospel is not mere miscalculation – it is heresy. Lowering Paul to the level of a novelist is bad enough, but raising anything to the level of the gospel violates the gospel.

I suppose someone in this wide world may have elevated corporate prayer to the level of the gospel. If so, I have never met that person. I have never been that person, and, by God's grace, I never will be.

It is wrong to make prayer a competitor to the gospel. It is also wrong to mischaracterize a persistent call to prayer as violating gospel territory. It was factually wrong to claim I put corporate prayer on the same level as the gospel. I never confused the gospel with anything we do. The gospel is news about what Jesus did. Period. The gospel has implications for what we do after we rely fully on what Jesus did, but what we do forms no part of the gospel.

I never preached about prayer as much as I did the gospel. Far from it. I preached about prayer when the text taught it (I preach expository sermons) or when dealing with church vision (which I cast), but not otherwise. I certainly never said corporate prayer took away our guilt and gave us good standing with God. Perish the thought!

I have, however, made a persistent call to prayer. My

persistence has been proper. Stubborn resistance made the ongoing call necessary.

My emphasis on corporate prayer applies the Lord's gospel to our Christian behavior. I call the group formed by the gospel to talk to the one who formed them as his people. Reflecting on the devotional behavior of the church following Pentecost, Michael Reeves comments, "Communal prayer, then, is the Christian life in a nutshell – the family of the Father coming together to him to share his concerns."[1]

Repeating pastoral exhortation does not trespass on gospel ground. The early church, for example, characteristically called for repentance and baptism. That emphasis did not lift repentance to the level of the bloody cross, or put baptism on the level of the empty tomb.

The accusation the pastor made is a poisonous fog. It can spread over all kinds of ground and attack any pastor attending to a pervasive problem in a local church. It attacks Paul and other apostles by implication.

Paul persistently corrected the Corinthians about disunity, selfishness, and sexual immorality. Should we charge Paul with placing unity, selflessness, and purity on the level of the gospel? Of course not. Paul applied the lofty gospel at the level of earthly behavior. Paul rebuked Peter for refusing to eat with Gentile believers in the Galatian church. Paul did not raise table fellowship to the level of the gospel; he called Peter to act in line with the gospel (Gal 2:14). Paul called for broad fellowship because of the gospel.

Corporate prayer is behavior befitting the gospel

because salvation produces supplicants. Consider an example from Judah's history. God addresses the exiles in Zephaniah 3:7-12.

> I thought: You will certainly fear me and accept correction. Then her dwelling place would not be cut off based on all that I had allocated to her. However, they became more corrupt in all their actions. Therefore, wait for me – this is the LORD'S declaration – until the day I rise up for plunder. For my decision is to gather nations, to assemble kingdoms, in order to pour out my indignation on them, all my burning anger; for the whole earth will be consumed by the fire of my jealousy. For I will then restore pure speech to the peoples so that all of them may call on the name of the LORD and serve him with a single purpose. From beyond the rivers of Cush my supplicants, my dispersed people, will bring an offering to me. On that day you will not be put to shame because of everything you have done in rebelling against me. For then I will remove from among you your jubilant, arrogant people, and you will never again be haughty on my holy mountain. I will leave a meek and humble people among you, and they will take refuge in the name of the LORD.

Some translations call the rescued exiles "worshipers" in v10. That is not wrong but it is not precise. Worship is a broad concept. The Hebrew term in v10 means to pray or entreat.

Prayer surrounds the verse in context. God's supplicants are worshipers, of course, but not all worship is supplication. The rescued people in this passage acknowledge God's greatness by calling on him as a community of faith.

The Hebrew phrase that says the rescued people will call on the Lord and serve him "with a single purpose" is literally "with one shoulder." In the Ancient Near East servants carried royalty on litters. Bearers had shoulders on the same level to serve as a team. The prophet employs an inherently corporate image for prayer.

Prayer by the disciplined Judean exiles did not compete with God's saving grace. Their united supplication manifested grace that the redeemed people cherished.

The same is true in the case of the church. Too many churches have many groups and ministries but lack one shoulder. God still expects redeemed supplicants to "wait for" him, to "take refuge" in him, and to "call on" him together in the "pure speech" of prayer as "meek and humble people."

Churches would do well to identify as bands of supplicants. We need one shoulder. We need to reclaim corporate supplication as an application of salvation received.

A church of supplicants united in pure speech glorifies God. How strange is it that a pastor's call to gospel-driven supplication should be cited as an intrusion into gospel turf? No one should wield the gospel-first motif like an axe to fell a pastor making proper application of gospel grace. So strong is the current resistance to a congregation praying as the body, a pastor or parishioner exhorting the church to pray corporately risks being labeled a gospel compromiser. Stunning.

The apostolic gospel and the priority of corporate prayer perfectly align as David F. Wells indicates.

> God-centered worship, no doubt, can be done in a variety of ways. However, it is what makes the people of God one, what makes them Christ's bride, his body, his flock that should be at the heart of what we do. These are the truths that make the church *the* church. There is only one God, only one Christ, only one cross, only one biblical Word, and only one gospel. These core beliefs were at the center of the early church's worship. Luke mentioned four activities within which these beliefs were affirmed. They were: first, 'the apostles' teaching'; second, 'fellowship'; third, 'the breaking of bread'; and finally, 'the prayers' (Acts 2:42).[2]

Prayer as the body expresses gospel life. William Willimon writes that Acts 2:42 displays, "a fourfold embodiment of the gospel."[3] A gospel-driven church will *not* be driven away from corporate prayer.

Let no one (pastor or otherwise) drive you (pastor or otherwise) from the priority practice of corporate prayer. Do not abandon this sacred duty. Remain patient and persistent as a humble advocate, even if you are falsely assessed. Sticks and stones may break bones, but disobedience harms the body.

PART THREE

PERSPECTIVE FROM PERFECTION

The song "The Word" by Sara Groves has an arresting verse.

> People are getting fit for Truth
> Like they're buying a new tailored suit.
> Does it fit across the shoulders?
> Does it fade when it gets older?
> We throw ideas that aren't in style
> In the Salvation Army pile
> And search for something more to meet our needs.[1]

Corporate prayer is not stylish, but it is scriptural. We consider some key Bible passages in this third part of our journey together. God's word is flawless. We must gain needed perspective from that perfection.

THE PROBLEM WITH TWO OR THREE

ook back over your school years. Did you dread any subject? For me, the clear answer is math. I am not a numbers person. I apologize to the math teachers who tried to help me, and to all others in the field. People like me are not your fault.

Math class tortured me even before algebra entered my life. Then a teacher hit me with $2+X = 4$. She dragged the alphabet into the mess! I won't talk about physics class, or I might suffer flashbacks and slip into the fetal position.

Some people like math, to which I say, "go figure." I am glad such people exist because if not, nothing would work. I promise to stay out of the way while they balance the books, design video games, or launch rockets. Even I, however, can handle $1+1 = 2$ and $1+2 = 3$. You can too. Let's take our mutual math prowess and turn it loose on a Bible text that people handle loosely, using it as a platform for corporate prayer.

Jesus said, "Again, truly I tell you, if two of you on earth agree about any matter that you pray for, it will be done for you by my Father in heaven. For where two or three are gathered together in my name, I am there among them" (Matt 18:19-20). It sounds like a call to have corporate prayer meetings. It seems to add the promise that Jesus will attend even if just two people attend a prayer meeting.

The passage does *not* function that way.

Go with the actual flow of the Lord's comments. Start with Matthew 18:15-20.

> If your brother sins against you, go and rebuke him in private. If he listens to you, you have won your brother. But if he won't listen, take one or two others with you, so that "by the testimony of two or three witnesses every fact may be established." If he doesn't pay attention to them, tell the church. If he doesn't pay attention even to the church, let him be like a Gentile and a tax collector to you. Truly I tell you, whatever you bind on earth will have been bound in heaven, and whatever you loose on earth will have been loosed in heaven. Again, truly I tell you, if two of you on earth agree about any matter that you pray for, it will be done for you by my Father in heaven. For where two or three are gathered together in my name, I am there among them.

The context is not about attending a prayer meeting; it is about paying attention to a deserved rebuke. It is not about a scheduled church meeting; it is about a sin problem.

Notice Peter's reaction in Matt 18:21-35.

Then Peter approached him and asked, "Lord, how many times shall I forgive my brother or sister who sins against me? As many as seven times?" "I tell you, not as many as seven," Jesus replied, "but seventy times seven. For this reason, the kingdom of heaven can be compared to a king who wanted to settle accounts with his servants. When he began to settle accounts, one who owed ten thousand talents was brought before him. Since he did not have the money to pay it back, his master commanded that he, his wife, his children, and everything he had be sold to pay the debt. At this, the servant fell face-down before him and said, 'Be patient with me, and I will pay you everything' Then the master of that servant had compassion, released him, and forgave him the loan. That servant went out and found one of his fellow servants who owed him a hundred denarii. He grabbed him, started choking him, and said, 'Pay what you owe!' At this, his fellow servant fell down and began begging him, 'Be patient with me, and I will pay you back.' But he wasn't willing. Instead, he went and threw him into prison until he could pay what was owed. When the other servants saw what had taken place, they were deeply distressed and went and reported to their master everything that had happened. Then, after he had summoned him, his master said to him, 'You wicked servant! I forgave you all that debt because you begged me. Shouldn't you also have had mercy on your fellow servant, as I had mercy on you?' And because he was angry, his master handed him over to the jailers to be tortured until he could pay everything that was owed. So also my heavenly Father will do to you unless every one of you forgives his brother or sister from your heart."

The Lord's statement about his presence comes in the middle of a passage that is, from beginning to end, about accountability. Jesus is present in the sanctified confrontation. The context concerns meetings in which believers confront a sinning brother or sister. Prayer fits the delicate process but is not the main point of the meeting.

Work the math about "two or three." Be daring and toss in the alphabet too. Do the work carefully to get the Lord's actual meaning as the product.

We start with the person sinning. We will label him person A. He does *not* count in the Lord's statement about "two or three." He counts as a person and matters as the cause of the meetings, but he is not at the meetings in the name of Jesus. He is there as a believer disobeying Jesus.

Next, we have person B. He lovingly confronts person A. Person B *does* count in the math of "two or three" because he works on behalf of Jesus. He calls the meetings in the name of Jesus, for the benefit of the sinner, and the health of the church.

The next two people also *do* count in the math. Person C comes into the mix if person A refuses to repent after person B confronts him. Person D might also help at the same time or in additional meetings.

The final person at the meeting is person J. I did not skip five letters – I used his initial. He is the only person identified by name. He is Jesus. He always counts most but does *not* count in the math of "two or three" because he is the one in whose name the duo or trio gathers. He rules in heaven but is spiritually present and engaged at the meetings.

Jesus spoke of the two or three who gather in his name. Persons B and C compose the "two" of this text. Add helper D and you have the "three" the Lord has in mind. The math is simple. It is a version of 1+1 = 2 and 2+1 = 3. Use the alphabet. B+C = "two" and B+C+D = "three."

The "two or three" are *not* at a standard prayer meeting. They *are* all on a sin cleanup detail. Someone sinned and did not ask for forgiveness. That is not why normal prayer meetings happen.

If the person had repented and asked for forgiveness right away, the gathering would not have taken place. Prayer meetings operate on a different basis. We do not see a single corporate prayer meeting in the New Testament called because a person sinned and would not repent.

It is great to know that the Lord is present with us when a small group of believers gather for prayer. That truth, however, is not the point of this passage. The Lord's words address the exercise of church discipline, starting with the actions of a few people and, if necessary, extending to the action of the body. The passage is about how a few faithful servants fit into the discipline ministry of a whole church.

The "two or three" serve as formal witnesses in a defined process. If the sinner refuses to repent, the witnesses take the matter to the larger body. If the confrontation stands on solid biblical grounds, the church prayerfully enacts discipline until the person changes course and asks for forgiveness. The Lord endorses the confrontation, the discipline, and the forgiveness.

The Lord did not make a promise about minimal prayer meeting quotas or pick random numbers. He linked this church discipline procedure with the Old Testament standard for multiple witnesses (Deut 19:15). He warned people who have been confronted not to take lightly the proceedings. To ignore deserved rebuke does not solve a problem; it adds another sin to a problem. It discounts the majesty and ministry of Jesus.

Jesus also warned about the problem of not forgiving a person who has repented. When a sinning believer has turned back to the right path, the church is obliged to forgive. That is where Peter got bogged down about the prospect of repeated mercy. Peter knew that the Lord's comments were not a platform for establishing prayer meetings. He did not ask, "How many prayer meetings should we have each week?" He asked, "How many times should I forgive?"

The passage does not teach about people talking to God in prayer meetings and God listening. It teaches about people gathering to talk about sin and the sinner listening or not listening. If the sinner is stubborn, the church listens to the problem, talks to Jesus, and acts with endorsement by Jesus.

Craig Blomberg calls our attention to the context and the language.

> Sadly, these verses have often been taken out of context and misused. It ought to be obvious that God regularly does *not* fulfill a promise like that of v.19 if it is interpreted as his response to any kind of request. In this context v.19 simply restates the theme of v.18. The word for any 'thing' (*pragma*) is a term frequently limited to judicial matters. Here Jesus reiterates that actions of Christian discipline, following God's guidelines, have his endorsement.[1]

The main praying group in the New Testament is in verse 17 – "the church." The main prayer arena is not a small circle of believers; the main prayer arena is the corpus. The "two or three" do not constitute a church or a corporate prayer meeting. They are a small task force working on an unpleasant assignment.

When we want to prove something important (like the crucial role of corporate prayer), we sometimes read favored ideas into Bible passages instead of reading the facts from the text. There are plenty of Bible passages that show corporate prayer is essential and mandatory for the church. We must not hijack passages that do not make that case.

The point of Bible study is not to *make* a point. The point is to *get* the point.

Matthew 18 is not saying that Jesus makes a special appearance at prayer meetings. The lesson is that we must confront sin in the church body, and to forgive that sin following repentance. Prayer plays a big role in doing that heavy lifting, but the passage plays no role in constructing the main platform for church prayer meetings.

The Lord's statement about being present is not a heart-warming line to cross-stitch and decorate prayer meeting rooms. It is a sober warning about the dangers of not repenting, and of not forgiving those who do repent. It is not intended to comfort us when prayer meeting attendance is low. It teaches us to do what is right, even if it feels uncomfortable.

Ten chapters later, in Matthew 28:16-20, the Lord makes a comment about his presence that applies to all situations.

The eleven disciples traveled to Galilee, to the mountain where Jesus had directed them. When they saw him, they worshiped, but some doubted. Jesus came near and said to them, "All authority has been given to me in heaven and on earth. Go, therefore, and make disciples of all nations, baptizing them in the name of the Father and of the Son and of the Holy Spirit, teaching them to observe everything I have commanded you. And remember, I am with you always, to the end of the age."

Jesus directs his church to obey all his orders. Those orders include two or three gathering for ongoing sin confrontation. His orders also include the body gathering for prayer. The Lord Jesus is always with his church. That is a fact. The question is, are we with him regarding confrontation and corporate prayer?

THING 1 AND THING 2

The crowd of graduating students showed respect but did not yearn to hear me speak. Officials invited me to talk at their public High School convocation. The audience wore a blank, ceremonial stare as I approached the podium. The polite crowd readied themselves to endure me. My first move surprised them more than the school had surprised me by providing a platform void of restrictions.

From my chino cargo pockets, I plucked the plush figures of Thing 1 and Thing 2. No one expected blue hair and red onesies that day! I said my first words, which follow.

The sun did not shine.
It was too wet to play.
So we sat in the house.
All that cold, cold, wet day.
I sat there with Sally.

We sat there, we two.
And I said, "How I wish
We had something to do!"[1]

Dr. Seuss did the job. Forty-four words (almost all single syllable) slew the blank stare. The graduates and their family members tuned in. I had them, and I told them about God's version of Things 1 and 2. The gambit was a guide to the gospel.

One day an expert in the Jewish law asked Jesus to name the greatest requirement. He wanted Jesus to tell him the most important thing to do. Jesus gave him a twofer. Matthew 22:37-40 reports the Lord's answer. "He said to him, 'Love the Lord your God with all your heart, with all your soul, and with all your mind.' This is the greatest and most important command. The second is like it: 'Love your neighbor as yourself.' All the Law and the Prophets depend on these two commands."

The Galilean carpenter who said, "Love the Lord your God," *is* God. He is God the Son. The one who said, "Love your neighbor" left glory to become our neighbor. God the Son added a full human nature to his full divine nature.

Why did he come? Because we all failed to love God fully, as required. We don't even have to review all Ten Commandments to see we are sinners. The prime sin is putting self before God. It leads to death.

We have *all* done it.

The gospel tells us what Jesus did to rescue sinners. Jesus put our self-inflicted wounds before his pleasure.

God the Son so loved God the Father that he lived in our sewer, yet he remained pure. On the cross, his clean hands embraced our worst problem. The sinless one paid for our sins, suffering divine wrath in our place.

Jesus did not quote the two Old Testament laws to provide a formula for self-salvation. Salvation only comes by trusting Jesus as Savior. The law depends on those two commandments; our salvation depends on Jesus alone. Christians can live the two priorities only because Jesus *has* saved us. God calls us to love him and to love others because Jesus *is* our life.

Corporate prayer is a prime way for the church to obey the two prime directives. In true corporate prayer, we put God first and others next. By praying when we don't want to, we die to self, love others, and love God.

Ephesians 5:1-2 says, "Therefore, be imitators of God, as dearly loved children, and walk in love, as Christ also loved us and gave himself for us, a sacrificial and fragrant offering to God." In the letter to the Ephesians, love and prayer are true partners. Paul reveals his labor of love for that whole body of believers in Ephesians1:15-19. He uses the following phrases: "I have not stopped giving thanks for you," "remembering you in my prayers," "I keep asking," and "I pray." In Ephesians 3:14-19 he mentions gospel-defined love three times. He also says, "I kneel," and "I pray."

Prayer *flows* from hearts when true love *fills* them.

The hatted cat in Sally's house caused havoc, aided and abetted by Things 1 and 2. The Lord's version of Things 1 and 2 play havoc with the self-centered household of the human heart. When saved sinners take them to heart, they put everything in proper order.

Keep perspective. We do not have to want to pray corporately. We do not even have to like praying corporately. The Bible does not place those requirements on us. We do *not* have to love corporate prayer, but we *do* need to love *by* corporate prayer. If we do, one thing is sure.

Jesus will love it.

FINDING FAITH

I am a Jersey boy, born and raised in the city of Newark. I lived in other Garden State neighborhoods too, but have not been a New Jersey resident since 1999. When I head back for visits, I wonder what I will find. How has the place changed? Is the Italian bread still amazing? How are the people I left behind? After you spend significant time in a place, you raise such questions as you anticipate your return.

The Son of God lived for a significant time here on earth. Jesus died on the cross for our sins, rose bodily from the dead, and ascended to glory. Before he left earth, he asked the same question I ask about my old neighborhood: what will I find when I return?

To find his question we go to Luke 18:1-8. When Jesus talks about "the Son of Man" he means himself as God's most special agent.

Now he told them a parable on the need for them to pray always and not give up. "There was a judge in a certain town who didn't fear God or respect people. And a widow in that town kept coming to him, saying, 'Give me justice against my adversary.' For a while he was unwilling, but later he said to himself, 'Even though I don't fear God or respect people, yet because this widow keeps pestering me, I will give her justice, so that she doesn't wear me out by her persistent coming.' Then the Lord said, "Listen to what the unjust judge says. Will not God grant justice to his elect who cry out to him day and night? Will he delay helping them? I tell you that he will swiftly grant them justice. Nevertheless, when the Son of Man comes, will he find faith on earth?"

Greek grammatical markers sometimes indicate whether the correct answer to a question is "yes" or "no". We look for the marker in the final question and we find... nothing.

Jesus answered the first two questions himself, but he let the last one hang unanswered. The question sounds pessimistic enough to make postmillennialists sing the blues! Not really. Jesus puts the question at the end of a parable intended to keep us from giving up. He implies that some *will* be looking up and praying hard.

Jesus is not a pessimist. He is a realist who knows faith is demanding and life is hard. He also knows that persistent prayer helps us handle hardship. The Lord calls us to be positive realists and not to give up. He lets this sobering question hang throughout history to make us contemplate his question over the long run.

To the despair of rabid atheists, humanity remains almost universally religious. Faiths abound, but Jesus means faith in the God of the gospel. Persistent prayer is the way faith manifests itself in the widow story. If an unjust judge answers a persistent request from a widow because it annoys him, then the Judge will answer persistent prayers from those he has justified because it pleases him.

Prayer in this passage seeks vindication in the face of opposition (see Rev 6:9-11 for an example from out of this world). The early church suffered many unjust attacks and responded with persistent prayer. If Jesus had returned right away, he *would* have found such faith in the Roman world. But Jesus did not return right away.

The Gospel of Luke and the book of Acts form a two-part record. As the story of Jesus and his church moves forward, the fellowship seeks justice from God during persecution. They do so by corporate prayer.

Consider one case. Opponents imprisoned Peter and John and ordered them not to preach the gospel as Acts 4:23-30 reports.

After they were released, they went to their own people and reported everything the chief priests and the elders had said to them. When they heard this, they raised their voices together to God and said,

"Master, you are the one who made the heaven, the earth, and the sea, and everything in them. You said through the Holy Spirit, by the mouth of our father David your servant: 'Why do the Gentiles rage and the peoples plot futile things? The kings of the earth take their stand and the rulers assemble together against the Lord and against his Messiah.' For, in fact, in this city both Herod and Pontius Pilate, with the Gentiles and the people of Israel, assembled together against your holy servant Jesus, whom you anointed, to do whatever your hand and your will had predestined to take place. And now, Lord, consider their threats, and grant that your servants may speak your word with all boldness, while you stretch out your hand for healing, and signs and wonders are performed through the name of your holy servant Jesus."

The church prayed *together* as *assembled* believers. Corporate prayer was the solution to persecution. Today if a pastor exhorts a church to pray corporately, some parishioners feel persecuted.

Enemies later tossed Peter back in jail. Acts 12:5 says, "So Peter was kept in prison, but the church was praying fervently to God for him." A prayer-driven miracle set Peter free from prison. He knew the body assembled to pray. He went to that meeting place.

The American evangelical church has imprisoned *itself* in prayerlessness. We have lost potency.

Acts 4 and 12 are direct applications of the widow story

Jesus told. The events recorded in Acts 12 happened well over a decade after Acts 4. The church had persisted in prayer. Borrow the Lord's words from the widow story: they did "not give up." A believer can make personal application of the widow and judge parable, but the corporate context was primary for the original disciples.

We have given up praying in the manner Jesus displayed in the widow parable in Luke 18. We have not applied the Lord's parable as the church did throughout Acts.

If the Lord Jesus returned today, would he find faith on the earth? Yes. He would find it in many persecuted churches.

The widow had one problem to bring before a court. When the judge dealt with it, the problem passed. She did not need to make further petition. The church, however, never passes beyond opposition in this world. So, petition to the highest court must not end in this world.

The Lord should find persistent prayer in every local church. Even where overt persecution is not present, this present world is not a friend to grace. Opposition to Jesus is the most unjust thing in the world. Faithful churches cannot dispense with prayers for justice.

Over my years as a pastor, many people have asked me about the churches I have served. The most common questions follow.

- How many people attend?
- What programs do you have for children and teens?
- What style of music do you use?

- What translation do you use?
- What are the staff positions?

I cannot recall anyone asking me how we prayed for the persecuted church. Our suffering brothers and sisters often fall off the American evangelical radar. No one ever asked how we prayed about justice in our land either.

Few people have ever asked how the body prayed about *anything*. Let that sink in.

We have focused on numbers, services, and styles. Prayer has faded. So many Christians are busy church window-shopping, we have forgotten the widow of Luke 18.

The world has various ways of leading us away from faithful dependence on God. If the world cannot persecute you to death, it will please you to death. Sometimes that way works best. The world relentlessly pursues us with its vision of the good life. We buy the comfy chair. We forget how to kneel.

The American media mildly attacks believers, but that is no big deal. More troubling is that they lure us to live by worldly values. It is more pleasant to have Madison Avenue after you than the secret police, but it is quite dangerous. The world's friendship can be more deadly to our spiritual life than its fury.

Where is the church weaker – where the world beats on it, or where the world seduces it? Where is the church praying most – in the comfort zones, or where persecution abounds? The worldwide persecuted church grows without religious freedom. The free American Church stagnates without corporate prayer. We must become better stewards of our freedom.

Ten chapters earlier in the Gospel of Luke, Jesus talked about *why* people turned away from him. Hear him apply the parable of the soils in Luke 8:12-15.

> The seed along the path are those who have heard and then the devil comes and takes away the word from their hearts, so that they may not believe and be saved. And the seed on the rock are those who, when they hear, receive the word with joy. Having no root, these believe for a while and fall away in a time of testing. As for the seed that fell among thorns, these are the ones who, when they have heard, go on their way and are choked with worries, riches, and pleasures of life, and produce no mature fruit. But the seed in the good ground – these are the ones who, having heard the word with an honest and good heart, hold on to it and by enduring, produce fruit.

If Jesus came back today, how rich a prayer crop would he find in your local church? Does your fellowship long for justice, especially for persecuted Christians? Does it plead for a harvest of souls? Does it pray for the further exaltation of Christ? Your practice of corporate prayer is your answer to those questions.

The Lord Jesus is coming back. When is he coming? That is the question we often ask. Some scan world news, looking for puzzle pieces to form guesses about the timing.

But we do not have to guess what Jesus wants.

Jesus looks for praying churches.

The body must persist in many kinds of prayers in addition to the cry for justice. We must confess sin. We must pray for each other and many others. We must thank God. We will eternally praise him, so praise must not fade in our corporate life now. If justice should make the church petition God, how much more should we praise him as recipients of eternal mercy?

Jesus is fully aware of all that is happening on earth. Before he ascended, he told the disciples, "I am with you always, to the end of the age" (Matt 28:20). Jesus need not return bodily to know what is happening on earth. Jesus is not puzzled about anything. He posed his question about finding faith because we often fail to be persistent. His question stands as a practical challenge to every local church. It also stands as a beacon of light in a dark world.

"Now he told them a parable on the need for them to pray always and not give up." Don't give up. Live up! Live up to your calling, church. Pray together as never before. The Lord will find faith in your assembly, and he will find it delightful.

THE REMAINING ISSUE

One childhood memory is so vivid I can almost taste it. The memory formed when this city boy visited relatives in a rural setting near Scranton Pennsylvania. I stood under a wine-grape trellis for the first time in my life.

My cousins and I picked and devoured the aromatic fruit. Then we discovered a trick that transcended culinary matters. That discovery carried us into combat. Squeezing the thick grape skin made the inside shoot out. That flesh could fly. We whipped off our shirts, and the battle was on. You have not lived until you've had grape innards plastered to your back at high velocity!

I enjoyed the snack and the silliness, but I missed the practical theology lesson right above my head. In Jerusalem, Jesus made the point I missed in Scranton. From him, the early disciples heard, through the grapevine, how real ministry works. John 15:1-10 tells us what Jesus said.

> I am the true vine, and my Father is the gardener. Every branch in me that does not produce fruit he removes, and he prunes every branch that produces fruit so that it will produce more fruit. You are already clean because of the word I have spoken to you. Remain in me, and I in you. Just as a branch is unable to produce fruit by itself unless it remains on the vine, neither can you unless you remain in me. I am the vine; you are the branches. The one who remains in me and I in him produces much fruit, because you can do nothing without me. If anyone does not remain in me, he is thrown aside like a branch and he withers. They gather them, throw them into the fire, and they are burned. If you remain in me and my words remain in you, ask whatever you want and it will be done for you. My Father is glorified by this: that you produce much fruit and prove to be my disciples. As the Father has loved me, I have also loved you. Remain in my love. If you keep my commands you will remain in my love, just as I have kept my Father's commands and remain in his love.

Grapevines did not often appear in my childhood neighborhood. A few trellises in scattered backyards hinted at homemade wine. But we did not see many grapevines in my urban setting.

The situation was different in the places where Jesus

taught. People often saw grapevines. A trellis might be located over his audience at times, but the vine illustration would not have gone over their heads.

Jesus used the common sight of vines to place himself in a unique position. He did not say, "I am a vine." He said, "I am the true vine." The church has only one source of life. Abraham, Moses, Peter, Paul – none of them is the vine. Jesus is the true vine because he is divine. He alone is true God in true human form. God the Father planted the vine when he sent his unique Son to live as a human on earth.

Disciples are the branches in that vine. Our fruit shows the life of Christ in us. God prunes fruit-bearing branches.

On the other hand, he cuts off every branch that bears no fruit and burns those branches. Jesus says those fruit-free branches are "in him." How can they be dead? Different kinds of connections are the key. The barren branches are not vitally connected to him.

This chapter comes between the Lord's prediction of betrayal and the terrible act. Judas had daily physical contact with Jesus as part of the Lord's small group. Judas velcroed himself to Jesus for a while. That connection is different than having the life of Christ coursing through you.

Today, people can be in a local church but lack the life of Christ in them. Without the life of Christ, church folk are still guilty sinners on the way to hell. The Father connects sinners to the Son by the work of the Holy Spirit. Only the Trinity can make eternal life. It is beyond our capacity to produce.

Our salvation is unearned, but it unleashes God's power in our lives. Paul made that clear in Ephesians 2:8-10. "For you are saved by grace through faith, and this is not from yourselves; it is God's gift – not from works, so that no one can boast. For we are his workmanship, created in Christ Jesus for good works, which God prepared ahead of time for us to do." The triune God's unique workmanship results in the good works true believers do.

God takes his time, and ours, to produce fruit. As the best gardener, God is patient. That truth should encourage believers who beat themselves up for being imperfect. I spent a good portion of my early Christian life in self-inflicted frustration. I had a hard time seeing the fruit in me that others saw. God's grace produces joy, not sour grapes.

Growth hurts sometimes. God prunes away disease. He removes even some things that are not bad but harm high yield. Good gardeners do that all the time; God does it because he is the best.

God prunes churches as well as individuals. The Lord presented his vine lesson, not to isolated individuals, but a band of disciples. The word "you" is consistently plural in this passage. The context concerns more than the moral virtue that Jesus produces in individual believers. It concerns fruitfulness in joint ministry. The church today must learn the lesson Jesus taught those disciples.

Jesus uses the word "remain" ten times in just seven verses in John 15 before he says "go." Remaining is the key. We cannot generate a good yield without remaining in

Jesus. In context, remaining means to seek him regularly by his word and prayer.

If we are going to be truly fruitful, we must face the *remaining* issue.

Too often in the evangelical church, we use prayer in snippets instead of remaining in prayer as a body. Prayer occupies the edges of our individual lives and church experience. We say grace at dinner, offer up a few lines at bedtime, and shoot up a desperate cry under duress.

Jesus directs the branches to ask. He calls us to be call-ers. As a band of disciples on a God-given mission, each local church must learn to *remain* in prayer. We cannot be fully missional if we are ommissional about corporate prayer. It is unwise to talk to people about God but fail to talk to God as his people.

The world does not need churches bursting with pro-grams and bustling to get great stats. It does not need churches always experimenting with the next new thing. The world needs churches that know how to remain. Our community, our friends, and our families need branches continually drawing life from the vine.

Draw near to God. Devour his word as eagerly as the shirtless boys of Scranton gobbled grapes. Ask grace to see God's excellence, and to display his glory in fruitful ministry.

Jesus said, "you can do nothing without me." He did not mean a church would either pray or stand stock still. His letters in Revelation 2-3 show fruitless churches can be a blur of activity. A church today can do many things without relying on Jesus. The members can work on curriculum, attend committee meetings, sing in music ministry, and yet not rely on God. As a trained technician, I can string words into a sermon without conveying the whole counsel of God and without crying out to God for his beloved sheep. I can even write a book in that mode. I did not, but I could.

Jesus insists, "you can do nothing without me." He means it. The Lord looks at our independent attainments and says, "that's nothing."

False success is the *most deceptive* form of failure. It keeps us from recognizing reality. The worst outcome is to have apparent success *without* prayer. It promotes unfounded confidence.

Go to a craft store and look at the rubber grapes. They are shiny and attractive and dead. Only God can make a living branch or a bunch of real grapes. Only God makes fruit with vitamins and juice.

Don't pile up rubber grapes in ministry. Produce real fruit. *More* is not better; *real* is better. Plans, programs, sermons, vision statements, and intentional ministry alone can never make a living branch with luscious fruit. Poet Joyce Kilmer wrote, "Poems are made by fools like me, but only God can make a tree."[1] Sermons and books are made by fools like me, but only God can make a real vine.

We need to remain always. Regardless of how well a church has done in ministry, there is room to grow. In the progression of the passage, Jesus moves from "fruit," to branches becoming "more fruitful," to branches bearing "much fruit." That is the Lord's church growth plan.

Churches that use business models emphasize inspirational pastoral leadership. The business world is most unlike the Lord's trellis teaching. What mere business CEO calls all his employees to remain in him? How, then, can any local church think it is effective if it relies on business models rather than remaining in the vine? How can we neglect to ask him for what we need through corporate prayer?

Ask him to prune away our prayerlessness, even if it hurts. If we fail to ask for all we need, we are simply asking for trouble. God designed a better outcome: joy for us and glory for him.

The big ministry issue today is the remaining issue. This lesson should not be over our heads. Jesus made it clear.

His practical theology lesson is more than a matter of life and death. Remaining is a matter of life, of more life, and of much life.

THE FIRST FOUR THINGS

magine this day's reading coming from me as a baseball manager. I hand the ball to Richard John Neuhaus as our starter. He winds up and deals.

Alfred Loisy, the nineteenth-century historian, was right in saying that Jesus came proclaiming the Kingdom of God but what appeared was the Church. The disappointment was, and continues to be, severe. But the great irony is that today we alleviate our disappointment with the contemporary Church by pointing back to the New Testament Church – which was the great disappointment to begin with! Our restless discontent should not be over the distance between ourselves and the first-century Church but over the distance between ourselves and the Kingdom of God, to which the Church, then and now, is witness.[1]

The current problem is not distance measured in time but devotion. We have distanced ourselves from a major way the first church bore witness to the kingdom – they talked to the King as his unified subjects. The coronation of Christ led them to corporate prayer.

We cannot be the early church. We should not try to defy irreversible chronology, but we *can* decide to pray as congregations. We can defy spiritual inertia.

Prayer by the body was one of the first four things the early church did to honor the Lord. Luke features that prime quartet in Acts 2:42. We touched on that in day nine's reading. The verse says, "They devoted themselves to the apostles' teaching, to the fellowship, to the breaking of bread, and to prayer."

No church has been perfect in *any* age, but churches can be healthy in *every* age. In Acts 2:42, Luke describes the church in a healthy state. His summary statement displays priority practices as a lasting example.

Bible commentator R. C. H. Lenski now comes onto the field as my middle innings pitcher. Listen to him depict Acts 2:42. "Here we have a brief description of the religious life of the first Christian congregation. All the essentials are present and are in proper order and harmony. The church has always felt that this is a model."[2]

My extensive research on Acts 2:42 confirms that his statement is accurate. Many scholars and church leaders across centuries point to Acts 2:42 as a model for indispensable church practices. The appendix of my book provides just a small sample.

Someone might balk and say, "Not so fast! What about Acts 2:44-45?" That section says, "Now all the believers were together and held all things in common. They sold their possessions and property and distributed the proceeds to all, as any had need." Why not see that form of money management as a mandate? Why focus on Acts 2:42?

The answer is that verse 42 forms the model. The verses that follow it display ways the church expressed the model.

Wise money management is a consistent biblical teaching. The communal form of property management found in Acts 2 (a voluntary approach which is *not* communism) does not appear after Acts 5. Corporate prayer is different because it is a normative practice in the remainder of the book (Acts 1:12-17; 2:1,41-47, 4:23-36; 5:12-14; 12:1-17; 13:1-3; 16:13-16; 21:1-6; 26:1-20).

At this point, I hand the ball to my late innings pitcher. Grant Osborne reaches back and delivers.

From the beginning, corporate prayer was the core of the early church's life. During the ten days in the upper room between Christ's ascension and Pentecost, we are told that the 120 "joined together constantly (lit. 'of one mind') in prayer" (Acts 1:14). The emphasis is on the harmony of the group and the unceasing nature of its prayers...The primary worship passage in Acts is 2:42-47, and in verse 42 Luke provides the "four pillars" of the earliest worship – teaching, fellowship, the breaking of bread, and prayer. It says the believers "devoted themselves" to these things, a critical concept in Acts (1:14; 2:42, 46; 6:4; 8:13; 10:7) that stresses both unity in pursuit of a goal and serious persistence in attaining these things.[3]

Someone opposed my call for corporate prayer by claiming that Acts 2:42 is descriptive, not prescriptive. Why would people dodge the clear implications and application of a passage from Acts by claiming it is just descriptive? Take, for example, Ananias and Saphira dying when they lied to the church. Are we to say, "Well, that is descriptive. It is not prescribing honesty; it is just describing what some people did in those early days. Therefore, we are free to lie to the church and provoke the Holy Spirit without consequence." Of course not.

Passages do not have to be prescriptive in their form to function as fundamental models. There are not many prescriptive passages in Acts, but there is much in the book we should emulate in the church today.

I could cite various examples from evangelical church practice where models are properly drawn from non-prescriptive passages. Consider just one case: the ministry of deacons. Churches today do not have deacons because a verse prescribes them by saying, "You must have the office of deacons in a local church. There is no prescriptive command about deacons like that anywhere in Scripture. Only qualifications for deacons are in a prescriptive form (1Tim 3:8-13), yet we properly perceive a model for our practice now in those early deacons.

I have seen many passages proposed as models for ministry. Some were reasonable applications of the text and others were not. How many times have you encountered people citing passages about corporate prayer while championing a ministry model? It seems that prayer is the sticking point for our selection of models.

All four elements in Acts 2:42 are prescribed in the Bible as church priorities. Would the pushback I experienced against the verse as a model have happened if corporate prayer was not in the four elements? I doubt it.

Pay attention to the way Luke uses articles, nouns, and plurals in Acts 2:42 to express exemplary behavior. Transferred *directly* into English, the Greek text says, "They devoted themselves to the teaching of the apostles, to the fellowship, to the breaking of the bread, and to the prayers."

The Greek text does not say, "some of them devoted themselves to fellowshipping." The definite article and noun combo ("the fellowship") points to people, not an activity. Fellowshipping is something people *do*; the fellowship is the *people* formed by what Jesus did. Fellowshipping can be done by some of the people; the fellowship is a congregation Jesus built.

The Greek text does not say, "some of the people did some praying." Scholars often write that the definite article and plural noun combo ("the prayers") indicates set prayer times for the church. The praying-as-the-fellowship team took the field first in church history. Where has it gone?

The word "together" occurs repeatedly in Acts 2:41-47 and forms the context for all four parts of Acts 2:42. They met together to listen to the apostles teaching, to eat the bread, and to function as the fellowship. A shift to solo or small group praying at the end of the verse does not fit. Prayer was not an optional program offered to especially devoted people. The devoted church practiced corporate prayer.

In recent decades, evangelicals have used Acts 2:42 as a model for small group ministries. The groups usually meet in homes, but some meet at a church facility. The groups often bear the label "242 Groups" even though they rarely practice the Lord's Supper. They often serve as the main place of prayer in a local church.

In Acts, the *whole* congregation was the 242 group.

The early church met in homes, but that does not mean the gatherings were like present-day small groups. Acts 1:13-15 shows a group of 120 people in a house meeting, which is about ten times the size of a typical small group today. Those house churches had elders, deacons, lists of widows, and a wide variety of spiritual gifts (1Cor 12, 1Tim 3-5). A home meeting was a congregation, not one church program among others.

When we seek a template for church-wide ministry, Acts 2:42 fulfills the quest. The early church won souls because of the basic disciplines of corporate prayer, obedience to God's word, celebration of the Lord's Supper, and loving one another as the Lord's fellowship. Acts 2:47 shows the payoff of their Acts 2:42 devotion saying, "Every day the Lord added to their number those who were being saved." It all started with the first four things.

Not three. Four.

One pastor said I made "a category mistake" when I used Acts 2:42 to call the church to corporate prayer. He meant that I put prayer in the category of the essentials of the faith. His mistake was thinking that corporate prayer is non-essential just because it is not in the same category as the deity of Christ or justification by faith alone.

Some things are essential for reasons other than defining core doctrine. Tooth brushing is essential for dental health. My toothbrush is not divine and cannot justify me. I still need it.

Corporate prayer is essential for church health. When we omit corporate prayer, we harm the corpus.

All four elements in Acts 2:42 are church behaviors *based on* doctrinal essentials. We are not free to neglect the Lord's Supper. We preach essential doctrines, but that does not make preaching a non-essential activity. Evangelism itself is not the gospel, but that does not make spreading the gospel optional behavior. Corporate prayer is, likewise, not optional.

The length to which even pastors go to let the church opt-out of a vital form of prayer frightens me. We have not been devoted to corporate prayer; we have demoted corporate prayer. If pastors spend as much time promoting corporate prayer in the future as they have spent excusing its neglect in the past, the church will be in much better shape.

We near the end of our imaginary baseball game. I call my closer from the bullpen. John Calvin takes the pitcher's mound to comment on Acts 2:42.

In these four things Luke describes the well-ordered state of the church. We must keep to these things if God and the angels are to judge us as the true church and not just boast to be such before men. Clearly, Luke is referring to public prayer. So, it is not enough for people just to pray at home by themselves, unless they also meet to pray, which is in itself a profession of faith.[4]

Imagine the American church behaving that way in the 21st Century. Don't imagine. Take the field as a real team and do it. It is still the winning formula. Don't take it from me – a make-believe baseball manager. The true team owner says so, and Jesus is the real deal.

TIME TO BE THE TEMPLE

You do not go into a donut shop to buy a lawnmower. You do not go into a hardware store to get a parakeet. You do not go into a pet store to find a cruller. Why not? Simple. You know what happens in each place. Your culture provides that knowledge.

The Ancient Near East had many temples. Everyone knew the normal activities found in temples. The Jewish people went to their temple in Jerusalem expecting certain features. Prayer was a primary activity there.

The priest Zechariah burned incense in the Jerusalem temple. That beautiful fragrance presented rising prayer. He did not do a solo act as a priest that day. Luke 1:10 tells us, "At the hour of incense the whole assembly of the people was praying outside."

Get the picture and live the lesson. Our assemblies should be a time of spiritual incense rising as we pray together.

Jesus knew prayer was a norm for temple ministry, as Luke 19:45-46 shows. "He went into the temple and began to throw out those who were selling, and he said, "It is written, 'my house will be a house of prayer,' but you have made it 'a den of thieves!'"

John 2:13-22 displays how much the violation disturbed the Lord.

The Jewish Passover was near, and so Jesus went up to Jerusalem. In the temple he found people selling oxen, sheep, and doves, and he also found the money changers sitting there. After making a whip out of cords, he drove everyone out of the temple with their sheep and oxen. He also poured out the money changers' coins and overturned the tables. He told those who were selling doves, "Get these things out of here! Stop turning my Father's house into a marketplace!" And his disciples remembered that it is written: "Zeal for your house will consume me." So the Jews replied to him, "What sign will you show us for doing these things?" Jesus answered, "Destroy this temple, and I will raise it up in three days." Therefore the Jews said, "This temple took forty-six years to build, and will you raise it up in three days?" But he was speaking about the temple of his body. So when he was raised from the dead, his disciples remembered that he had said this, and they believed the Scripture and the statement Jesus had made.

The one who drove those people out of the temple was not into consumer-driven ministry. Zeal consumed him.

The Lord's zeal led him to act like a hawk toward the dove-sellers. He was not in a bad mood that day; he was in a devotional state of mind. Jesus said, "The one who sent me is with me. He has not left me alone, because I always do what pleases him" (Jn 8:29). The prayer-driven whipping Jesus administered was no exception.

Why were those offenders in the temple precincts? They performed a service for the worshipers. Some replaced currency from wide-ranging places with quality silver for the temple tax. Others provided ritually pure animals. If a family came from far away, it was not convenient to drag even a ritually clean animal to the festival.

If these money men performed a necessary service, why was Jesus angry? They should have done the work outside of the temple court. Even if they did not cheat people, they failed to keep a respectful distance. The sound of moos and moolah competed with the prayers. Jesus was justifiably angry at the disharmony, and he elected to become the house whip.

The Messiah put down his whip, got whipped, was crucified, died, and was entombed. He came out of the tomb on Easter morning. He raised the temple of his body to build a related temple that will last forever. The eternal temple based on the Lord's work is the church. It has no courts separating Jews and Gentiles, or men and women. We are one in Christ as a living temple.

In 1Corinthians 3:16-17, Paul pictures a local church as

a temple. "Don't you yourselves know that you are God's temple and that the Spirit of God lives in you? If anyone destroys God's temple, God will destroy him; for God's temple is holy, and that is what you are." This passage does not identify a believer's physical body as a temple (as in 1Cor 6:18-20) but identifies the church as a temple.

Paul does the same thing in 2Corinthians 6:16. "And what agreement does the temple of God have with idols? For we are the temple of the living God, as God said: 'I will dwell and walk among them, and I will be their God, and they will be my people.'" In Ephesians 2:21-22 Paul again speaks about the church as a temple. "In him the whole building, being put together, grows into a holy temple in the Lord. In him you are also being built together for God's dwelling in the Spirit."

The Bible shows the living temple visiting the stone temple. Acts 2:46 says, "Every day they devoted themselves to meeting together in the temple." They went there for prayer. Two verses later in Acts 3:1 we read, "Now Peter and John were going up to the temple for the time of prayer at three in the afternoon." Paul talks about praying at the Jerusalem temple as a Christian in Acts 22:17.

The church expanded beyond Jerusalem, so the eternal temple did not always meet at the time-bound one. In 70AD the Romans destroyed the stone temple. The living temple continued being a house of prayer.

You know what to expect in a donut shop, a hardware store, and a pet store. What do you expect to find in a local church? How high is corporate prayer on your list of expectations? How zealous are you to find it?

We behave destructively toward the temple when we neglect to pray together. D. A. Carson gives a sobering warning.

> The ways of destroying the church are many and colorful. Raw factionalism will do it. Rank heresy will do it. Taking your eyes off the cross and letting other, more peripheral matters dominate the agenda will do it – admittedly more slowly than frank heresy, but just as effectively on the long haul. Building the church with superficial 'conversions' and wonderful programs that rarely bring people into a deepening knowledge of the living God will do it. Entertaining people to death but never fostering the beauty of holiness or the centrality of self-crucifying love will build an assembly of religious people, but it will destroy the church of the living God. Gossip, prayerlessness, bitterness, sustained biblical illiteracy, self-promotion, materialism – all these things, and many more, can destroy a church. And to do so is dangerous: "If anyone destroys God's temple, God will destroy him; for God's temple is sacred, and you are that temple (1Cor. 3:17)".[1]

Jesus cleansed the Jerusalem temple *for* prayer, but we have purged the living temple *of* prayer. Jesus used his body to turn *over* tables, but we have turned *from* prayer as the body. The money changers robbed *others*, but we have robbed *ourselves*.

It is time to turn the tables on ourselves. It is time to be the temple.

DISSECTING A JAILBIRD'S JOY

A deft stroke slid the scalpel into the exposed stomach. My premier as a surgeon proceeded calmly for two reasons: I was working on a frog, and the frog croaked long before I met him.

My high school thought that seeing the belly of the beast would enrich my life. Our biology teacher directed us to name our specimen. We bestowed his name based on a discovery. Tiny pinchers tumbled from the open organ, so we dubbed him "Claws." If consuming crayfish claws is a frog's life, then it's not easy being green.

Nor being an apostle. Especially the one named Paul.

His ministry often made him a jailbird. One year, he perched in a Roman prison waiting to see if Nero would order severe neck surgery. A messenger named Epaphras arrived from distant Colossae. His report about his home church made prisoner Paul rejoice despite the shadow of

Nero's sword.

What could be that great? Paul explained in Colossians 2:1-5.

For I want you to know how greatly I am struggling for you, for those in Laodicea, and for all who have not seen me in person. I want their hearts to be encouraged and joined together in love, so that they may have all the riches of complete understanding and have the knowledge of God's mystery – Christ. In him are hidden all the treasures of wisdom and knowledge. I am saying this so that no one will deceive you with arguments that sound reasonable. For I may be absent in body, but I am with you in spirit, rejoicing to see how well ordered you are and the strength of your faith in Christ.

The jailbird sang for joy because a church was *orderly*!

Have you ever rejoiced because a church was well-ordered? If you faced a death sentence, would you rejoice in an orderly church? Finding crayfish claws in a frog's gut is no surprise compared to finding this odd clause in Paul's letter. Let's dissect this strange delight.

Imagine people gushing about the church they attend. Which of the following seems likely?

- Come to our church. You will love it – the people are friendly.
- Come to our church. You will love it – the music is wonderful.
- Come to our church. You will love it – the teaching is solid.

- Come to our church. You will love it – the youth pro-gram is exciting.
- Come to our church. You will love it – the church is well-ordered.

One of these things is not like the others. I doubt you have heard the fifth statement. What did Paul see that we miss?

Paul did *not* rejoice that the congregation had well-proofed bulletins free of Comic Sans font. He did *not* thrill to their impeccably groomed ushers marching like a drill team. He *did* rejoice because he saw the gospel in their hearts and actions. Their gospel-formed order helped change the Roman world.

We derive joy from order in various ways. Order is the precision of a Bach Fugue. It is Michelangelo's David and Winslow Homer's watercolors. It is a Shakespeare sonnet. Order is the Fischer vs. Spassky chess championship (only on the board) or a serious game of Chutes and Ladders. Order turns burning nitro into dragstrip thrills. It is a power-play rush from goal line to goal. Order is a proper German Chocolate Cake.

Order is your skeleton. If it becomes rigid, you lose free-dom. But lose your skeleton and you get nowhere baking a cake, skating, or driving a dragster. One of my comic role models was WABC radio disc jockey, Dan Ingram. One day he read a supermarket commercial for boneless chuck, paused, and said he knew the fellow – they carried him around in a dishpan. Boneless church is as lame as Boneless Chuck. Legalists turn order into a disease, but their move does not make good order bad. God gave the church good bones so we can go places.

The triune God displays ordered relationships. The Spirit makes the Son known, the Son made salvation, and the Father made the plan. Delight yourself in the Lord and you delight in his kind of order.

God ordered his creation, separating night from day, land from sea, and one species from another. He gave his moral law. We cannot break it without the loss of peace and the gain of pain. Order is pristine Eden. Disorder is people idolizing money, possessions, and power. It is lust, gossip, slander, theft, drunkenness, lying, cheating, idolatry, sexual immorality, hatred, murder, selfishness, and self-righteousness. Disorder leads to the final High Court appearance and the ultimate death sentence.

But there is good news. Order is Jesus who lived perfectly under the moral law. He thirsted, bled, and died before a bloodthirsty mob. In so doing, he planted order in chaos. Jesus rose and will return to spread resurrection glory everywhere.

Jesus saves sinners one by one so we will live as an orderly body. Colossians speaks to a church and speaks to us as the church. Individualism is out of order. Christian community is the order of the day.

Paul's delight was formed by theology and informed by a threat. The Colossian church held their position under pressure from their culture and from false teachers who claimed to be Christian. Their order conformed to the truth.

The Greek term for "well-ordered" is *taxin*. Romans used it for troops in proper formation, prepared for action. Paul wrote this letter while chained to a Roman soldier. Perhaps he turned to the guard and said, "What is that battle formation you use? That's just the word for the church in Colossae."

The word "strength" here is *stereoma*. Romans used it for an army that presented a firm front. Paul saw the church standing firm against the onslaught of untruth, for the sake of the lost.

The word for "struggling" is *agona*. Romans used it when people engaged in a contest like wrestling. How could Paul fight hard for the Colossians in a prison cell 900 miles away as the crow flies? He struggled for them by prayer. He stood on the battle line with them, firing off petitions and thanks. The related participle *agonizomai* occurs as "wrestling" in Colossians 4:12-13. Paul tells the church, "Epaphras, who is one of you, a servant of Christ Jesus, sends you greetings. He is always wrestling for you in his prayers, so that you can stand mature and fully assured in everything God wills. For I testify about him that he works hard for you, for those in Laodicea, and for those in Hierapolis." The messenger agonized with them on his knees.

The whole church body must join the prayer struggle. Listen to Paul's congregational prayer call In Colossians 4:2-6.

Devote yourselves to prayer; stay alert in it with thanksgiving. At the same time, pray also for us that

God may open a door to us for the word, to speak the mystery of Christ, for which I am in chains, so that I may make it known as I should. Act wisely toward outsiders, making the most of the time. Let your speech always be gracious, seasoned with salt, so that you may know how you should answer each person.

A well-ordered church does more than *organize* ministry, fine as that is. It *agonizes* in prayer.

In Ephesians 6:8-20, Paul gives the Ephesian church another group summons in the great armor passage. "Pray at all times in the Spirit with every prayer and request, and stay alert with all perseverance and intercession for all the saints. Pray also for me, that the message may be given to me when I open my mouth to make known with boldness the mystery of the gospel. For this I am an ambassador in chains. Pray that I might be bold enough to speak about it as I should." The words "pray at all times" cannot mean "feel free to stop praying when you assemble."

Prayer is essential for spiritual combat. Yet, the struggle is not real in many congregations. We have a first world problem – overreliance on organization. We must redeploy the first-century solution – corporate prayer.

I have spent years wrestling with church members and leaders who resist corporate prayer. Paul would find their resistance strange. A prayer-deficient church is out-of-order even if it is organized. Being out-of-order is deadly when so much is on the line. We must return to prayer.

Churches delight people with varied activities, engaging speakers, and extravaganzas. Some of those things are fine in their place. None can replace a phalanx of believers praying in good order.

I left Claws the frog pinned to a waxed lab tray in my biology classroom. Has my life been rich because I saw his stomach? Not really. Church life is rich when we practice corporate prayer. I see that now. I will keep calling the church to pray until I croak, and graduate to a far richer life.

HOUSEHOLD CHORES

Hydrogen gas is extremely flammable. Do not smoke near it!

So said the instructions that came with our water heater. The manufacturer provided instructions because the company cares about us. I presume they also fear lawyers.

God fears none, but he loves us and instructs the church he made. God's servant Paul gave divine directions to a young pastor in 1Timothy 3:14-15. "I write these things to you, hoping to come to you soon. But if I should be delayed, I have written so that you will know how people ought to conduct themselves in God's household, which is the church of the living God, the pillar and foundation of the truth."

Paul intended the message of 1Timothy to apply to a whole local church, not just to a pastor. The letter was not a classified document. Timothy read it to the church he served. It teaches lessons about the role of whole churches.

Builders use pillars and foundations to counteract downward forces that would topple a structure. Each local church must support the truth by holding it up for all to see. The recipients of this letter lived near one of the seven wonders of the world. The magnificent Temple of Diana featured 127 massive marble pillars. The Ephesian congregation got the picture Paul drew.

The Greek text rendered *directly* into English says, "you will know how people ought to conduct themselves in God's household, which is church of the living God, pillar and foundation of the truth." The idea is not one pillar holding up lots of truths, but many churches holding up the one message of Christ.

God does not picture the church as customers sitting at Starbucks with lattes, enjoying speculative schmoozes about this or that. God pictures us as pillars of the truth. It is not arrogant to preach the truth; it is arrogant to say there is no truth. We defy Jesus if we deny the truth is real. He did not come to debate interesting ideas, give mere opinions, or provide clever conversation starters. He came to earth as "the way, the truth, and the life" (Jn 14:6).

The Bible commands the church to stand for truth. It commands us to pray as a household so we can live aligned with truth. Part of the non-negotiable truth is that prayer by the church is crucial for the life of the church.

1Timothy 3:14-15 stands near the center of the letter, and reveals the heart of the letter. Home is where the heart is, and the heart of this letter is God's house. The household image puts a fine point on the family image. Relatives can be scattered all over; a household has a definite location. This letter explains how a local church must behave to be a healthy household.

If my wife and children never spoke to me while we were all together, our household would be strange. The same would be true if only one of them spoke to me while we were all together. If one of them refused to speak to me while the others were present, I would be alarmed. Why do we think it is normal to gather as God's household, yet only one or two do all the talking to our Father? Why do some believers think it is normal to never speak to God during family time?

God's household is formed by grace, yet he sets household chores. The chores are reasonable and good for all. Some prime examples appear in 1Timothy 2:1-4. "First of all, then, I urge that petitions, prayers, intercessions, and thanksgivings be made for everyone, for kings and all those who are in authority, so that we may lead a tranquil and quiet life in all godliness and dignity. This is good, and it pleases God our Savior, who wants everyone to be saved and to come to the knowledge of the truth."

How often do we reflect those priorities as we meet? Why neglect practices that please God? Why don't we all pray so we all achieve the goal (godliness) of life?

Throughout this letter, God's word and prayer appear as priorities. For example, 1Timothy 4:4-5 says, "For everything created by God is good, and nothing is to be rejected if it is received with thanksgiving, since it is sanctified by the word of God and by prayer." If a church preaches nice stories but neglects the word, it violates house rules. If a church has lots of activity but neglects prayer, it commits the same violation.

Legalism is not the point. The household rules are not human-generated laws and do not make you a member of the family. They are guidelines for grace-based living *as* the family. Parents appreciate it when children do their tasks willingly and for the good of all. So does God.

When we veer from God's directions, we end up in hot water. When a church is faithful as God's household, living water flows and many people benefit. Each church can thrive. Thank God for that truth. We can do well even in hard times and places. The Ephesian church lived in an idolatrous environment that was hostile to godliness. If the word and prayer were effective there, they will be effective anywhere and anytime. They will always be far more effective than anything we devise.

Return to the water heater in my basement. The manual warned my family not to remove any instructions or labels. It said we could be injured or killed if we handled the heater carelessly. So much is at stake in my basement!

When it comes to the church, the stakes are infinitely higher. Souls are at stake. Health is at stake. Joy is at stake. True worship is at stake. God gave his household permanent instructions so we thrive. We cannot afford to remove any of them, including the call to corporate prayer.

I never smoke near my water heater. I appreciate the manufacturer's instructions, and I respect the destructive power of hydrogen gas. I do not want to destroy my household.

As the household of God, do we respect his instructions? God the Father sent God the Son. God the Son died and rose for us, and sent the Holy Spirit. God the Holy Spirit moved Paul to write so the church would know what is good and true.

If the Triune God went to all that trouble for us, at least we can do our chores for him.

PRAYER AND THE WORSHIP LEADER

n common evangelical lingo, "Worship Leader" desig-
nates a song leader. The label often indicates a church
staff member. Do you think Jesus should bear the label?

"Worship Leader" fits him supremely. His blood positions the church for life-wide worship. The book of
Hebrews says much about that. It pictures Jesus as leading
congregational praise, and it links his unique position with
our prayers as his body.

Consider some passages to see the link. Pay close attention to the flow and the context.

Start with Hebrews 2:5-10, which talks about God the
father making the Son the supreme ruler.

For he has not subjected to angels the world to come
that we are talking about. But someone somewhere
has testified: "What is man that you remember him, or

the son of man that you care for him? You made him lower than the angels for a short time; you crowned him with glory and honor and subjected everything under his feet." For in "subjecting everything" to him, he left nothing that is not subject to him. As it is, we do not yet see "everything subjected" to him. But we do see Jesus – made lower than the angels for a short time so that by God's grace he might taste death for everyone – "crowned with glory and honor" because he suffered death. For in bringing many sons and daughters to glory, it was entirely appropriate that God – for whom and through whom all things exist – should make the source of their salvation perfect through sufferings.

No one else has suffered more, or accomplished more than Jesus has on our behalf.

Next consider Hebrews 2:11-18, which puts Jesus at the head of our worship.

For the one who sanctifies and those who are sanctified all have one Father. That is why Jesus is not ashamed to call them brothers and sisters, saying: "I will proclaim your name to my brothers and sisters; I will sing hymns to you in the congregation." Again, "I will trust in him." And again, "Here I am with the children God gave me." Now since the children have flesh and blood in common, Jesus also shared in these, so that through his death he might destroy the one holding the power of death – that is, the devil – and free those who were held in slavery all their lives by the fear of death. For it is clear that he does not reach out to help angels, but to help Abraham's offspring. Therefore, he had to be like his brothers and sisters in every way, so that he could become a merciful and faithful high priest in matters pertaining to God, to make atonement for the sins of the people. For since he himself has suffered when he was tempted, he is able to help those who are tempted.

Jesus is not *a* worship leader. Jesus is *the* Worship Leader.

Focus on five themes from Hebrews 2:5-18 and trace them forward in the letter. They reveal a profound link between our Worship Leader and corporate prayer.

First, believers are a "congregation." We are a family. The source of our salvation gathers us under his direction and sets us on a course of worship. The passage speaks of the congregation as "the people," "many sons and daughters," "brothers and sisters," "the children" and talks about what we have "in common."

Second, God the Father "crowned" the Son with glory. Jesus rules over all things and people. Who else but God could bring many children to glory? God the Son will do it by his superior sovereignty.

Third, Jesus provides "help." As Lord, he does not play the part of a lackey. The recipients of this letter knew from the Old Testament that God was Israel's helper, yet God is no one's valet. God the Son stooped to become a servant, but he never became a stooge. We have the supreme helper.

Fourth, Jesus is also our "high priest." He disposes of sin and dispenses mercy. He showers humble, yet confident, supplicants with grace.

Fifth, the text highlights being "tempted." The author encourages a church under persecution. Their hostile culture tempted them to cave in. Enormous pressure bore down on them to abandon the faith. They needed top-notch help to stand firm and tall.

Keep those five themes in mind: the congregation, Jesus crowned as Lord, the help he provides, his role as high priest, and our being tempted. Now move forward in the letter.

Watch the themes reemerge in Hebrews 4:14-16.

Therefore, since we have a great high priest who has passed through the heavens – Jesus the Son of God – let us hold fast to our confession. For we do not have a high priest who is unable to sympathize with our weaknesses, but one who has been tempted in every way as we are, yet without sin. Therefore, let us approach the throne of grace with boldness, so that we may receive mercy and find grace to help us in time of need.

Here again, Jesus is Lord, he is a high priest, temptation is a big problem, and Jesus provides big help. The early church would notice the reemergence of the themes from chapter two.

They would also remember the teaching about the congregation. When the author says, "we," "us," "our," the pronouns evoke the "congregation," "the people," "many sons and daughters," "brothers and sisters," "the children," and what they share "in common." All those corporate elements were in chapters two and three. Individual devotion has not replaced them in chapter four.

In the ancient world, congregations gathered to hear letters like this read aloud. Only a few minutes of reading stand between chapter two and chapter four. If you listen to the letter read aloud in English, Hebrews 4:14 comes about six minutes after you hear Hebrews 2:18.

An average baseball inning takes about twenty minutes. Do we forget what happened at the top of the inning when we reach the bottom? No. It takes less than half that time to move from chapter two to chapter four. The church heard the thought-flow. Recitation was common in that culture, and people listened well.

How well do we read? If we isolate verses, we miss a lot. Common courtesy says we must pay attention to what a person communicates. Ripping statements out of context bothers people. We must bother to follow the Holy Spirit's orderly writing.

The word "prayer" does not appear in Hebrews 4:16, but the context indicates that prayer is the way to appear before the throne to find help. People often apply Hebrews 4:16 to personal prayer, which is fine. I do it myself. It is great to know I can take my frailty and sin to the throne of grace. It is not good, however, to miss the corporate context.

Hebrews 4:16 calls a congregation to pray. To claim that corporate prayer is not essential, you must practice inattentive reading or interpretive gymnastics. We must not miss the thematic consistency of chapters two through four. We can make individual application of the text, but sound interpretation emphasizes the corporate reality.

If you listen to the letter read aloud, Hebrews 5:7 comes about 90 seconds after Hebrews 4:16. The themes of the high priest, temptation, prayer, and help appear again. Observe Hebrews 5:7-11.

> During his earthly life, he offered prayers and appeals with loud cries and tears to the one who was able to save him from death, and he was heard because of his reverence. Although he was the Son, he learned obedience from what he suffered. After he was perfected, he became the source of eternal salvation for all who obey him, and he was declared by God a high priest according to the order of Melchizedek. We have a great deal to say about this, and it is difficult to explain, since you have become too lazy to understand.

Are we stronger than the incarnate Lord? Do we prioritize prayer because we are wise like him? Real humans need to pray. Jesus came as a human to save us by grace, and to glorify his Father in heaven. He did that perfectly, in large part, because he prayed. Don't minimize the Lord's prayer life.

During World War II, the British Army in North Africa hid tanks underneath wood and canvas structures. The top part looked like a real truck. They could move armor around disguised as mere truck traffic. I fear some Christians think that way about Jesus. "He looked like a real truck, but we know underneath he was a tank. He enjoyed success in ministry because of all that divine firepower concealed under that canvas cover." That bad theology is a disservice to Jesus. He prayed as a service to God and us.

Jesus prayed and he expects his church to do the same. He is never lazy. He is patient, but he sets limits to delayed discipline (Heb 12-13). Let's not test his patience further by our lack of congregational prayer.

Are we stronger than brothers and sisters around the world who live by corporate prayer? A friend of mine met an African couple who immigrated to the United States. They wondered why they did not find corporate prayer in our churches. They said that the church in Africa often did not know where the next meal would come from. The congregation seriously prayed, "Give us today our daily bread" (Matt 6:11).

My son taught the Bible to South Sudanese refugees in Uganda. The assembly praised God and pled his blessings in a modest structure in the hot savannah. Their name for the Sunday service is "Prayers." Some of those believers lost all their worldly goods but kept their perspective on prayer and worship.

In a doubly different climate, the sign in front of an American church invited people to join their Sunday services. The sign said, "Worship with us – our services are air-conditioned!" That church featured AC but not CP. I have no problem with air conditioning. I have a big problem with the world conditioning us to omit corporate prayer.

The persecuted church prays together around the world. Their physical and spiritual lives depend on it. That is the context of the invitation to approach the throne of grace in Hebrews 4.

Just because we have different circumstances in the United States, we do not have permission to put prayer on the periphery. Curtis C. Mitchell reminds us that we are always in danger.

A person in trouble will not only pray but he will also pray in dead earnest. A man with his car stalled on the railroad tracks with a train approaching won't look on prayer as a nice religious exercise. I'm sure we can all testify to the fact that our most effective times of prayer have been when we are in big trouble. Remember how effectively you prayed in the ambulance as they were rushing your child to the emergency room at the hospital? The only problem is that *we are always in trouble*, but we are too blind to realize it! Each day we are involved in a titanic struggle with unseen yet real forces (see Ephesians 6:12). We are called upon to do battle daily with the world, the flesh, and the devil. We've got the world that's *external*, the flesh that's *internal*, and the devil who's *infernal* to deal with every day of our lives! If we could actually see the hellish hoards round us each day, we would be panicked into fervent prayer![1]

Don't wait for the imagined panic. Accept the real invitation to pray from Hebrews 4:16.

The American church does not risk life and limb as worshipers, yet we trifle with a culture that worms its way into mind and heart. An ancient snake is behind the insidious worm. Congregations still need to pray, "deliver us from the evil one" (Matt 6:13). We need to pray that to honor the Worship Leader.

Approaching a local church for what services you can get from it is a world apart from the corporate worship in Hebrews. Jesus looks for a congregation that approaches his throne for all it needs. The best Worship Leader is not on any church staff – he is the church's Savior. Jesus is omnipotent and sympathetic to our weakness. He set the example of praying through temptation, and he saved us so we could follow his lead.

The world is a wilderness of temptation. Don't worry. Pray. Strength for the day is ours always, through the one who is always the same. All we have to do is follow the Leader.

TEN PASSAGES TO PONDER

We conclude part three of this book with a high-speed survey of passages. The following texts speak (one way or another) to the importance of corporate prayer. I encourage you to study all ten passages in context. Don't stop with these texts. Survey the whole New Testament with eyes open wide to the praying body.

Plurals in the Prime Prayer

"Therefore, you should pray like this: Our Father in heaven, your name be honored as holy. Your kingdom come. Your will be done on earth as it is in heaven. Give us today our daily bread. And forgive us our debts, as we also have forgiven our debtors. And do not bring us into temptation, but deliver us from the evil one" (Matt 6:9-13). What has tempted evangelicals to forsake those plurals?

Another Lord's Prayer

"I pray not only for these, but also for those who believe in me through their word. May they all be one, as you, Father, are in me and I am in you. May they also be in us, so that the world may believe you sent me. I have given them the glory you have given me, so that they may be one as we are one. I am in them and you are in me, so that they may be made completely one, that the world may know you have sent me and have loved them as you have loved me" (John 17:20-23). When we refuse united prayer as the body, we work against the Lord's prayer.

The Waiting Room

"They all were continually united in prayer, along with the women, including Mary the mother of Jesus, and his brothers" (Acts 1:14). They had a world to win for Jesus, but Jesus commanded them to wait. The world-reaching church was born in a prayer-rich waiting room.

Kid's Stuff Too

"When our time had come to an end, we left to continue our journey, while all of them, with their wives and children, accompanied us out of the city. After kneeling down on the beach to pray, we said farewell to one another and boarded the ship, and they returned home" (Acts 21:5-6). The report is about a church body, including children, praying as one. How often today does a local church mirror this cross-demographic behavior?

All and All and All

"Pray at all times in the Spirit with every prayer and request, and stay alert with all perseverance and intercession for all the saints" (Eph 6:18). Ephesus was a Roman colony and its people knew that Roman soldiers interlocked their shields to accomplish their mission. "Pray at all times" *cannot* mean "neglect praying in gathered times." Pray with "every prayer" *cannot* mean "omit corporate prayer."

Free to Pray

"Don't worry about anything, but in everything, through prayer and petition with thanksgiving, present your requests to God" (Phil 4:6). While applicable to individuals, this verse is about the body. It calls a persecuted church to pray. Religious freedom has lured us into prayerless ministry.

Direction for Devotion

"Devote yourselves to prayer; stay alert in it with thanksgiving" (Col 4:2). Paul directed this church body to pray as the church did in Acts 2:42, using the same Greek word for "devote." Are we such devotees?

Characteristic Corporate Prayer

"See to it that no one repays evil for evil to anyone, but always pursue what is good for one another and for all. Rejoice always, pray constantly, give thanks in everything; for this is God's will for you in Christ Jesus" (1Thess 5:15-18). Corporate prayer is good for all, and Paul wanted it to characterize worship gatherings. "Pray without ceasing" (KJV) cannot possibly mean "cease praying together."

The Good Fight

"What is the source of wars and fights among you? Don't they come from your passions that wage war within you? You desire and do not have. You murder and covet and cannot obtain. You fight and wage war. You do not have because you do not ask" (Jas 4:1-2). Church fights are much more common than are churches fighting the good fight by united prayer.

Satisfaction vs. Sardis

"Write to the angel of the church in Sardis: Thus says the one who has the seven spirits of God and the seven stars: I know your works; you have a reputation for being alive, but you are dead. Be alert and strengthen what remains, which is about to die, for I have not found your works complete before my God. Remember, then, what you have received and heard; keep it, and repent. If you are not alert, I will come like a thief, and you have no idea at what hour I will come upon you" (Rev 3:1-3). For all our lively ways, the American evangelical church lacks a reputation for corporate prayer. Is Jesus completely satisfied, or are we Sardis?

Just a Sample

I cannot establish the historical facts, but I heard the following story. Queen Victoria was in a church service. She liked short sermons. After the service, the preacher asked what Her Majesty thought of the sermon. She said, "You were brief." He replied, "I do not like to be tedious." She told him, "You were also tedious."

Perhaps some readers will find this day's nerve-touching reading tedious. The survey could have been much longer. It is only a sample. Maybe Victoria's conversation with the preacher never happened, but Jesus is in our churches every week. He loves to hear corporate prayer.

His Majesty cannot get too much of it.

PURSUING PRAYER

Part three demonstrated from Scripture that corporate prayer is a priority for the local church. In part four, we deal with obstacles to practicing communal prayer. We also explore ways to seize opportunities to pray as God's people.

THE BIG BULLY

No one likes a bully. But what do you do when the bully is the very thing that allows you to like, dislike, or be ambivalent about something? What if the bully is *emotion*?

Our feelings are great when smelling roses, hearing symphonies, or watching the long ball soar into the upper deck. But emotions are not all sunshine and daffodils. Our feelings shove us around sometimes. They love to bully us concerning prayer by the body. Schoolyard bullies threaten us with bodily harm. When we allow feelings to keep us from corporate prayer, we harm the body of Christ.

I find it much easier to preach a sermon to the church body than to sit quietly with the body in prayer. Writing a book on corporate prayer is easier than practicing it. That says a lot. Writing is hard, but time flies for me. That is not usually the case in corporate prayer. Quieting my restless soul is a challenge. If I let my feelings rule, I would not practice what I am preaching.

Feelings must not rule. My friend rarely feels like cooking, but she has three children. They must eat to be healthy and grow, so, she is compelled to cook. Prayer is no less important for a growing church body.

Our feelings about prayer are tricky. We feel that we should like corporate prayer, but we do not. So, we feel guilty. We feel we should be able to pray as freely as others seem to, but we cannot. So, we feel like failures. We feel we should not have so much trouble quieting our unruly hearts and minds, but we do. So, we feel frustrated and decide to quit.

Then Satan has us right where he wants us.

C. S. Lewis used fictional letters to express a real problem. Screwtape (a senior demon) writes to a novice tempter, training him to undermine prayer by believers. "Teach them to estimate the value of each prayer by their success in producing the desired feeling; and never let them suspect how much success or failure of that kind depends on whether they are well or ill, fresh or tired, at the moment."[1]

Who said you must always feel fine for prayer to work? Who said emotional baggage is not allowed at a prayer meeting? Who said you must like prayer meetings? Who said you must have a prayer style like someone else?

The Stoic philosopher Epictetus could stay flat emotionally. One day his master forcefully twisted Epictetus' leg. The slave told his master, "If you continue to do that, you will break my leg." Sure enough – snap! Know what Epictetus calmly said? "Didn't I tell you that you would break my leg?"[2]

Scripture does not advocate Stoicism. Abraham, the paragon of faith, mourned his wife Sarah's death (Gen 23:2). The suffering psalmists often cried out "why?" (Psa 10:1; 22:1; 42:5,9,11; 43:2; 44:23, 24; 74:1; 80:2; 88:14). Godly men grieved deeply over the martyrdom of Stephen just days after the resurrection of Jesus (Acts 8:2). The Galatians angered Paul by defecting from the faith (Gal 3:1-3). Paul said Epaphroditus' death would have caused him sorrow upon sorrow (Phil 2:27). He wrote about the ministry provoking his tears, anguish, and despair (2Cor 1:89; 2:4).

Jesus was not a stoic either. Jesus was frustrated with his disciples for their amazing lack of insight (Matt 17:14-16). He cried at the grave of his friend Lazarus (Jn 11:35). He sweat blood in Gethsemane as he prayed (Lk 22:39-46). On the cross, he asked "why?" which is the big question sufferers ask (Matt 27:46).

God gave us emotions. In a fallen world, feelings can go haywire. At times we should feel lousy. But we have no reason to give up because we feel weak.

Weakness is a *prime reason* to pray.

Exercise discretion in corporate prayer. Details of sin and struggles are not necessary. Some information will not be appropriate for all to hear. Prudence is part of prayer in the fellowship.

Stop letting emotion shove you around. Let the whole schoolyard take on the brute together. Gang-up in sanctified fashion. The bully looks like a giant but is not as tough as we imagine.

Listen to Charles Spurgeon's advice about cmotions. "We should pray when we are in a proper mood, for it would be sinful to neglect so fair an opportunity. We should pray when we are not in a proper mood, for it would be dangerous to remain in so unhealthy a condition."[3] The great preacher knew more about prayer than I do, but I am not convinced that being in a non-praying mood is so dangerous. Thinking we should never feel that way is quite dangerous.

In a perfect world, we would never be blasé, but in this fallen world, it happens. Decide to move forward. Don't just emote. Think clearly. Rely on sound theology. Will. Act. God is bigger than the bully, and he gladly helps those who express their need before his throne.

Pray through your emotions. Don't let them prey on you.

THIS THING DOES NOT WORK

Why isn't the word "phonetic" spelled phonetically? Why isn't there a synonym for "thesaurus?" Why doesn't the word "palindrome" read the same backward? Those standard bits of humor indicate that we live in a world with irony.

Want more irony? Pragmatism does not work.

Pragmatism means taking the "practical" approach. That makes sense to a degree. I am typing this sentence with my fingers rather than with my nose. It is especially wise that I do so because my allergies are in full bloom. Who knows what I might write with an allergic nose?

I do not advocate impracticality. It is quite practical to realize that what works for one task will not work for another. We need to choose the approach that fits a given task. Fingers are good for typing, but you cannot use them to stop and smell the roses.

We need to stop. Something is rotten in Denmark (if you say that in Denmark, blame it on Shakespeare). Something smells in the American Church.

Pragmatism pollutes our atmosphere. We need church climate change.

Decades of pragmatic approaches to church growth have not worked. More people are delighting in large churches, but there are not more church devotees. No study I have seen shows a surge in spiritual growth or numeric increase.

The early disciples devoted themselves to prayer, and the church grew spiritually and numerically. The fellowship did not come up with that plan. They did not say, "Hey, this prayer thing we created might just work." They prayed together because they were obedient to the Lord. Corporate prayer is a God-given tool for a God-given task.

God has always done things differently than humans. Consider what God said to the people of Judah in Isaiah 55:6-8.

Seek the LORD while he may be found; call to him while he is near. Let the wicked one abandon his way and the sinful one his thoughts; let him return to the LORD, so he may have compassion on him, and to our God, for he will freely forgive. "For my thoughts are not your thoughts, and your ways are not my ways." This is the LORD'S declaration. "For as heaven is higher than earth, so my ways are higher than your ways, and my thoughts than your thoughts."

Pragmatism is a philosophy from the lowlands. Lord, plant our feet on higher ground.

God rebuked his people in Isaiah 31:1-3 for aiming too low.

> Woe to those who go down to Egypt for help and who depend on horses! They trust in the abundance of chariots and in the large number of horsemen. They do not look to the Holy One of Israel and they do not seek the LORD. But he also is wise and brings disaster. He does not go back on what he says; he will rise up against the house of the wicked and against the allies of evildoers. Egyptians are men, not God; their horses are flesh, not spirit. When the LORD raises his hand to strike, the helper will stumble and the one who is helped will fall; both will perish together.

They should have said, "whoa" to the chariot horses. They did not. So, God pronounced "woe" on his beloved people.

God is good, but he is not sentimental. He is sensible and spots sin every time.

The chosen people went down to Egypt, not just directionally or topographically, but spiritually. They went west, back to their former masters, and failed to please their true master. They paid a steep price. Eventually, God sent them many miles east to Babylon for seven decades of therapy.

The point is not that chariots are bad. David and Solomon had plenty of them. *Relying* on chariots is bad.

Using helpful tools is reasonable; replacing the ultimate helper with tools is madness. The people forgot how God liquidated the chariots that chased Israel out of Egypt. They forgot how God freed them through a series of miracles. The escapees did not work a way out. God did the impossible. The people thought making bricks without straw was hard. Try making the exodus without God.

The church faces a fierce challenge. Leaving Egypt is one thing, but reaching the world is another. The church must meet the mission with prayer. For us, prayer is a practical tool for the job. The assigned task is beyond our best ideas and efforts. I cannot type with my nose, but we can take the high road on our knees.

S. D. Gordon explained the right approach. "You can do *more* than pray *after* you have prayed but you can *not* do more than pray *until* you have prayed."[1] When you must do what you cannot do, the first thing to do is pray.

The church is free to use tools like social media, demographic studies, strategic planning, curriculum, and programs. I have driven all those chariots and will continue to do so as appropriate. But none of us is free to put tools in God's place or to replace the spiritual tools our Sovereign has given his church.

I fear that the reason we do not pray as the body is that we do not believe prayer works. At one level, prayer does not work. Isaiah 1:15 proves the fact. God tells his people, "When you spread out your hands in prayer, I will refuse to look at you; even if you offer countless prayers, I will not listen. Your hands are covered with blood." Prayer does not work when we welcome sin. The Bible shows that sins other than bloodshed can negate prayers (Prov 1:24-31; Jer 11:10-14; Mal 1:7-10; Matt 6:5; Jas 4:3; 1Pet 3:7).

Prayer *itself* does not work; God works *through* prayer. He works through prayer when his people are humble. We lack humility if we tell ourselves that prayer simply does not work. God disagrees.

We must not pick up prayer occasionally and then toss it aside when we do not see the results we want, as quickly as we want. Do not trivialize corporate prayer with a tepid trial and then cry out, "this thing does not work," as if prayer is a broken remote control. Pragmatism is the thing that does not work for the ministry. It cannot move mountains. No idol can. Toss it.

Corporate prayer will work, in God's time, because it is his *way*.

Archimedes wanted a large enough lever to move the world. We have it. Only the church has the tool of corporate prayer, and it is one of the best levers ever. Why do we let the tool gather dust? We need to put down the chariot reins for a while, and take up the precious tool of united prayer.

Pragmatism is about doing what works. But what do you do when what "works" is not working? If you are wise, you rɪˈpɛnt. I used the phonetic spelling to make it easier for us all.

TO BUY OR NOT TO BUY?

You hear a sound – perhaps of sonar pinging or a dog barking. The sound comes from your pocket. In the past, that would baffle people, but you know what it means. You just received a text message.

A close friend texts, "Let's do lunch. I am dying to see you. We will meet at your place if that is OK with you." So far, so good. Then your friend writes, "Thinking about you is like having a nasty taste in my mouth that makes me want to spit." Sounds bad. Why would any friend say that?

Jesus sent a similar text to a church. He was their closest friend. The Lord loved them to death, but he said they made him want to spit. Why?

We find the Lord's message to that church in Revelation 3:14-22.

Write to the angel of the church in Laodicea: Thus says the Amen, the faithful and true witness, the originator of God's creation: I know your works, that you are neither cold nor hot. I wish that you were cold or hot. So, because you are lukewarm, and neither hot nor cold, I am going to vomit you out of my mouth. For you say, "I'm rich; I have become wealthy and need nothing," and you don't realize that you are wretched, pitiful, poor, blind, and naked. I advise you to buy from me gold refined in the fire so that you may be rich, white clothes so that you may be dressed and your shameful nakedness not be exposed, and ointment to spread on your eyes so that you may see. As many as I love, I rebuke and discipline. So be zealous and repent. See! I stand at the door and knock. If anyone hears my voice and opens the door, I will come in to him and eat with him, and he with me. To the one who conquers I will give the right to sit with me on my throne, just as I also conquered and sat down with my Father on his throne. Let anyone who has ears to hear listen to what the Spirit says to the churches.

Laodicea had no major historical accomplishments and was not a great city. Location, location, location was the selling point. It sat right on a vital communication and trade route. Commerce ruled. People knew the city for banking, black wool, and medical services – especially the production of eye salve.

Jesus sent letters to seven churches in Asia Minor (Rev

2-3). The Lord gave an entirely negative review to only one church of the seven. Laodicea was that church and was the only boastful church of the seven. The letter must have shocked them. Perhaps they wondered if Jesus sent them the wrong letter. They thought they had a spit and polish church. In a way, they got it half right. Jesus wanted to spit.

Do you know about syrup of Ipecac? Doctors use it to make people vomit. In medical terms, it is an emetic. In the Greek text, Jesus tells the Laodiceans they make him want to *emesai*. The notoriously bad water in their city had that effect on people. Their fellowship had that effect on Jesus. Jesus is always the most pointed with people who are the most prideful.

Jesus explicitly tells this church his love leads to his discipline. As Jesus wrote about spitting them from his mouth, his hands, feet, and side bore the marks of his crucifixion. No one loved them more.

The Lord uses Laodicea's strengths to rebuke the church: money, garments, and ophthalmology. He offered them better gold, eye salve, and garments. He calls them to buy his spiritual resources: righteousness, purity, and insight.

What currency could they use to make the crucial purchases? God told the answer to the self-reliant kingdom of Judah in Isa 55:1. "Come, everyone who is thirsty, come to the water; and you without silver, come, buy, and eat! Come, buy wine and milk without silver and without cost!" In Isa 55:6-7 the prophet says, "Seek the LORD while he may be found; call to him while he is near. Let the wicked one abandon his way and the sinful one his thoughts; let him return to the LORD, so he may have compassion on him, and to our God, for he will freely forgive."

Humble prayer is the proper tender for God's people in *any* era. Forms of money come and go and values fluctuate. Real prayer *never* loses value.

Jesus called the Laodicean church to repent. For a church to repent, a church must pray. You can always bank on repentant and dependent prayers.

In Revelation 3:20 Jesus knocks on the church door. The congregants inside enjoy a nice dinner and congratulate themselves on their fine church. The door verse is not about evangelism; it is about Christians welcoming Jesus to church. Doing church in style was not enough for the Savior; someone inside needed to start the repentance. All needed to join.

Like their city, the Laodicean church loved being self-sufficient, comfortable, and mediocre. They were too much like their culture to provoke a negative reaction from it. They only managed to provoke a negative reaction from the Lord.

The American church has more physical, economic, and informational resources than anyone in history. We have many good tools, but we also face a trap. We can be so enamored with our cultural resources that we put a stop order on corporate prayer. We need to stop stopping.

Repentance is not just an individual matter. The Lord's letter to Laodicea shows that whole local churches can repent. Sinclair Ferguson correctly observes, "Repentance is worked out both inwardly and outwardly in entire communities of believers."[1]

Why don't we go to the throne together to repent? Are we afraid God might renovate our churches to his taste?

The churches in Smyrna and Philadelphia fared well in the Lord's review. Those churches were a buyer's market. Jesus still has the goods today.

To buy or not to buy? That is the question. What answer does your church give Jesus?

CHURCH LEADERS DON'T WANT TO...BUT MUST

The setting: a Bible college campus. The characters: an older student and yours truly. The bottom line: discomfort for both and change for me.

Here is how the real-world drama went. I was being a smart aleck. The older student confronted me even though we did not know each other well. He told me that he respected my abilities, but that I had a habit of behaving like an immature dolt. That stung!

The episode was no fun for him or me. After the initial shock, I took his words to heart. He was right, and I had to deal with that. I started to change for the better that day.

Why didn't my friends and acquaintances say what I needed to hear? Why him? He had courage and he cared. He had nothing to gain personally. I did. So, he rebuked me as a service to me.

In 2Timothy 4:1-2, Paul told his pastoral protégé,

Timothy, "I solemnly charge you before God and Christ Jesus, who is going to judge the living and the dead, and because of his appearing and his kingdom: Preach the word; be ready in season and out of season; rebuke, correct, and encourage with great patience and teaching." Paul did not tell him to encourage, encourage, encourage and to do nothing else but encourage others.

Consider what Paul told another protégé. In Titus 2, the apostle gave young pastor Titus practical examples of godliness: showing self-control, being sensible, loving others, being respectable, being submissive to authority, behaving reverently, enduring, being faithful, denying worldly desires, and being eager to do what is good. In Titus 2:15 he then said, "Proclaim these things; encourage and rebuke with all authority. Let no one disregard you."

The consumer marketing model does not encourage pastors to rebuke people. Rebuke does not sell. Walmart does not reprove me if I fail to meet their expectations. They know I don't like to be rebuked, so they only woo me. The church, however, is a different matter altogether. Shepherds must know that rebuke is part of the package. Pastors should spend less time reading about influencing, motivating, and exciting people. We should spend more time fortifying our practical theology of pastoral rebuke.

Of course, no leader should start with rebuke. But what happens if we lovingly and patiently call a church to prayer and get stonewalled over time? Do we dare to employ even a *mild* reproof? Would we ever offer a strong rebuke over corporate prayer? If not, why not?

We should not want to rebuke the flock. Anyone who likes rebuking people is warped.

Take Jeremiah as an example. He did not want the rebuking job, but he did the job. He was not a philosophical pragmatist, calculating the odds and concluding that correction would work out happily for all. He did the job as a faithful prophet under orders to tell the truth.

God indicated Jeremiah's rebukes would not work out happily. He told the prophet, "When you speak all these things to them, they will not listen to you. When you call to them, they will not answer you. Therefore, declare to them, 'This is the nation that would not listen to the LORD their God and would not accept discipline. Truth has perished – it has disappeared from their mouths'" (Jer 7:27-28). Pragmatism and prophetic ministry cannot be partners.

We pastors should not *want* to rebuke the flock, but we must have the *will* to do so when proper. We spend years getting to know a congregation. Do we love the flock as much as the mere acquaintance who lovingly corrected me in Bible college?

I have never seen a book on corporate prayer that deals with rebuke. In 2Timothy 3:16-17, Paul tells pastor Timothy, "All Scripture is inspired by God and is profitable for teaching, for rebuking, for correcting, for training in righteousness, so that the man of God may be complete, equipped for every good work." Do we think rebuke is antiquated equipment? Do we respect the authority of God's word?

William Willimon provides perspective to timid preachers by way of a memory.

I recalled a wonderful comment by Walter Brueggemann, something said to us preachers like, "If you are a coward by nature, don't worry. You don't have to be courageous to be a preacher. All you have to do is to get down behind the text. You can say, 'This is not necessarily me saying this – but I do think the text says it.'" We can hunker down behind the text! Disjointed from service to the text, all I can do is to serve the congregational status quo, run pastoral errands for the world as it is, rather than let God use me to create a new world. And that is not only no fun; it's also immoral. I must make clear in my preaching that I preach what I have been *told* to preach. I serve the text, not those who listen.[1]

I take his point. We serve the flock by serving the text first.

We pastors seem to think we can always woo people, but God says sometimes we must rebuke them. Many of God's servants in Scripture rebuked faithfully even when they saw no immediate results. Do we have that kind of resolve?

How many members of a church will receive a rebuke from a pastor in the right manner? Psalm 141:5a says, "Let the righteous one strike me – it is an act of faithful love; let him rebuke me – it is oil for my head; let me not refuse it." The demographic group that shops for reproof is tiny and has always been that size. That is one reason Paul commanded pastors to be courageous.

When is the last time you heard an evangelical

pastor rebuke a congregation about *anything*? Paul told Titus to reprove believers who adopted the lazy ways of their Cretan culture. In Titus 1:12-13 he tells Titus to rebuke them "sharply." Have you ever heard a pastor deliver even a mild reproof to a church that was lazy regarding prayer?

Abraham Lincoln wrote, "Men are not flattered by being shown that there has been a difference of purpose between the Almighty and them."[2] Pastors know that correcting people is a dangerous career move. But a pastor has a divine calling, not a mere career. The real danger is refusing pastoral obligations.

A leader correcting a church, when appropriate, chooses to protect the flock instead of protecting his ego and security. A leader who refuses to teach the truth and confront excuses is a LINO – Leader In Name Only. If shepherds do not love the flock enough to rebuke it when needed, we do not love the flock enough.

Jesus is the ultimate example. He asked his disciples what the polls said about his real identity. The disciples reported that some people said Jesus was the return of Jeremiah the prophet (Matt 16:13-14). Think about that.

Jeremiah irritated practically everyone. Jeremiah described himself as "a man who incites dispute and conflict in all the land" (Jer 15:10). His rebukes infuriated people. The more the prophet reprimanded God's people, the more his ratings tanked. He hit bottom in a muddy water tank thanks to an irate audience.

The polls said Jesus might be Jeremiah making an

THE CORPORATE PRAYER CHALLENGE

encore. The Good Shepherd kept talking the hard talk and walking to the cross. Crucifixion was the most terrifying spectacle of the ancient world. It was a bloody, brutal mess. Jesus hit the ultimate bottom when the irate mob killed the Messiah. The unseen burden of our sin was the worst part of his plunge.

The Lord had a divine calling, not a mere career. He cried over the city he rebuked (Lk 19:41-44). Then he died for sinners like me. Am I willing to die to self in all aspects of my pastoral calling? If you are a pastor or are preparing to be one, do you?

Jesus set his face like flint toward Jerusalem. His approach resonates with the poem "The Flint" by Christina Rossetti.

An emerald is as green as grass,
A ruby red as blood;
A sapphire shines as blue as heaven;
A flint lies in the mud.
A diamond is a brilliant stone,
To catch the world's desire;
An opal holds a fiery spark;
But a flint holds fire.[3]

The Palestine crowds did not desire rebuke, but Jesus made fire that purifies. In the name of the flint-faced Savior, we pastors need to be less like sparkling baubles and more like spark-stones.

TURN, TURN

Lennon and McCartney. Arlen and Mercer. Rogers and Hammerstein. Gilbert and Sullivan. King and Goffin. Menken and Ashman. Gershwin and Gershwin. Sherman and Sherman. Many songwriting duos have trod the world's stage. Perhaps the most unusual duo is Solomon and Seeger.

King Solomon and Pete Seeger lived a millennium apart. Seeger adapted Ecclesiastes 3 by Solomon for the song "Turn, Turn, Turn" in the 1950s. The Byrds covered the song in 1965, and it reached #1 on the Billboard Top 100. Despite the mass appeal of "Turn, Turn, Turn," the masses did not turn to the eternal God who moved Solomon to write.

Solomon wrote about time and life in Ecclesiastes 3:1-8.

There is an occasion for everything, and a time for every activity under heaven: a time to give birth and a time to die; a time to plant and a time to uproot; a time to kill and a time to heal; a time to tear down and a time to build; a time to weep and a time to laugh; a time to mourn and a time to dance; a time to throw stones and a time to gather stones; a time to embrace and a time to avoid embracing; a time to search and a time to count as lost; a time to keep and a time to throw away; a time to tear and a time to sew; a time to be silent and a time to speak; a time to love and a time to hate; a time for war and a time for peace.

Bring Isaiah on stage now. He lived between Solomon and Seeger. The prophet knew his day was a time for love, even though the people of his day did not applaud the way he expressed love. He told hard truth about how God's people loved to turn, turn, turn from God. Judah had formed a discordant duo with Egypt instead of trusting God. Isaiah's audience probably wanted to throw stones at the prophet. Perhaps some did.

In time, God would kill. God eventually used the Babylonians to destroy the temple and carry a remnant of his beloved people into exile.

The prophet sounded the warning about misplaced confidence and the consequences. Isaiah 30:1-7 samples the way Isaiah rocked the world of Judah.

Woe to the rebellious children! This is the LORD'S declaration. They carry out a plan, but not mine; they make an alliance, but against my will, piling sin on top of sin. Without asking my advice they set out to go down to Egypt in order to seek shelter under Pharaoh's protection and take refuge in Egypt's shadow. But Pharaoh's protection will become your shame, and refuge in Egypt's shadow your humiliation. For though his princes are at Zoan and his messengers reach as far as Hanes, everyone will be ashamed because of a people who can't help. They are of no benefit, they are no help; they are good for nothing but shame and disgrace.

Zion trusted in Zoan. They thought relying on Egypt was realpolitik. God called it rebellion.

Observe the audience reaction to faithful prophets in Isaiah 30:10-11. "They say to the seers, 'Do not see,' and to the prophets, 'Do not prophesy the truth to us. Tell us flattering things. Prophesy illusions. Get out of the way! Leave the pathway. Rid us of the Holy One of Israel.'" The Hebrew text says, "Stop from our face the Holy One." Isaiah, and other faithful servants, showed them more God than the people wanted to see.

Isaiah stayed on the assigned path in his decades-long run. In the end, the people killed the prophet. Tradition says they sawed him in half. Stones sound better.

For all his rebukes, Isaiah preached hope through repentance. Isaiah 30:15-16 says, "For the LORD GOD, the Holy One of Israel, has said: 'You will be delivered by returning and resting; your strength will lie in quiet confidence. But you are not willing.' You say, 'No! We will escape on horses' – therefore you will escape! – and, 'We will ride on fast horses' – but those who pursue you will be faster." The word for "turning" is the word for repentance.

They refused to repent. God charged them with *resisting rest*. The punishment shows the crime was serious.

The supreme Judge delayed executing the sentence for a time. A miracle saved the capital in Isaiah's day. God sent the Assyrians away in a panic, and he patiently gave his people time to reconsider their stubbornness. Judah learned nothing. Eventually, Egyptian Rahab led Judah to Babylonian rehab.

Punishment is not God's petulant pleasure. God's justice and compassion are in harmony. Even the exile was mercy. He disciplined them by justice because of his compassion. He gave them the *bread* of adversity, not the *stone* of adversity. He nourished holiness by discipline.

Isaiah 30:18-21 signals a bright prospect with tones of both justice and mercy.

> Therefore the LORD is waiting to show you mercy, and is rising up to show you compassion, for the LORD is a just God. All who wait patiently for him are happy. For people will live on Zion in Jerusalem. You will never weep again; he will show favor to you at the sound of your outcry; as soon as he hears, he will answer you. The LORD will give you meager bread and water during oppression, but your Teacher will not hide any longer. Your eyes will see your Teacher, and whenever you turn to the right or to the left,

your ears will hear this command behind you: "This is the way. Walk in it."

The individuals who first heard that message died long before those blessings came to Judah as a people. God's plans transcend a generation. Some 700 years before Isaiah served, Moses explained how the exile would work. You can read all about it in Deuteronomy 28.

The exiles finally turned back to God. It was a time to heal. In 1Corinthians 10, Paul said those people serve as a warning for the church. God takes his time, and his people's time, to produce holiness. Only he knows how much time we have to process the lessons we must learn.

American evangelicalism does not cry, "Let's go down to Egypt." We come close, though, by crying, "Let's go to the next hot seminar. Let's devour the latest books. Let's mimic the successful churches." We trust in practical things like demographics, promotion, strategy, and vision. We kick up dust, and corporate prayer disappears.

We have resisted rest. I aided and abetted by attractive programming positioned to compete with prayer. As I confessed earlier, I have repented.

I call the church to repentance about corporate prayer because I love the church. The call wins little applause, but no one has thrown stones yet or picked up a saw. I want all to discover, as I have by grace, that our strength is found in repentance. It is the best rest of all. Prayer produces activity, but not frantic and fruitless action. Rest begets real progress.

Judah foolishly turned to Egypt and paid a steep price. Then Judah wisely turned to God by humble prayer and gained much.

It's our turn now. Which turn is it for you?

THREE STEPS FORWARD

My sister and I made a road trip to an unfamiliar part of Pennsylvania to attend a family party. Afterward, we got onto Route 80 to head back home to New Jersey. We were absorbed in conversation until we realized (after traveling about an hour) that we should have seen the Delaware Water Gap. Like hitting a deer in the fast lane, we ran smack into the truth. Our home was east, but we were on Route 80 West!

We had to change our minds about our true bearing. It was time for a 180-degree turn. We rode an hour simply to get back where we had started. The Beach Boys "Sloop John B" was playing and made us smile when we heard, *"This is the worst trip I've ever been on."*[1]

In truth, the worst trip I've ever been on was when I was a lost sinner heading away from God. Pleasant as my trip was in many ways, I was heading toward hell. But God allowed me to see my true position. The truth about my sin hit hard, but it was good for me.

Repentance is not just for sinners asking for salvation. When the church goes astray, we must turn back to the one who has saved us. It is the kind of turn Jesus demanded from five of the seven churches in Revelation 2-3.

We have strayed from the proper course for prayer. So, we need to take three steps.

Repent

The first step is to repent of our neglect of corporate prayer. Turning back is moving forward; holding the course is futile. My sister's van was going fast but we were not on the right vector. If we were stubborn, we would have never reached home. Motion does not always mean progress.

The American church machine is going full bore, but are we making progress? A. W. Tozer bemoaned the busyness in his day.

> Right now we are in an age of religious complexity. The simplicity which is in Christ is rarely found among us. In its stead are programs, methods, organizations and a world of nervous activities which occupy time and attention but can never satisfy the longing of the heart. The shallowness of our inner experience, the hollowness of our worship, and that servile imitation of the world which marks our promotional methods

all testify that we, in this day, know God only imper-
fectly, and the peace of God scarcely at all.[2]

Tozer wrote those words in 1963. The situation has not
improved.

Tozer asked the church a question that remains timely.
"When will we come to the point of repentance, throw all
the excuses out the window and fall on our faces before
God and an open Bible? When will we repent of our sin
and allow the Holy Spirit to do whatever the Holy Spirit
wants to do?"[3]

Repentance is the simple solution. Ministry books
often feature complex models and matrices. Cumbersome
graphs and graphics supposedly chart the way forward.
No. We simply need to turn back to God's way.

Endure

The second step is to endure. If my sister and I turned in
the right direction for a few miles and then went back in the
wrong direction, we would have wasted even more time.
In Acts 2:42, the Greek word for "they devoted themselves"
means a single-minded commitment to a course of action. (If
you are a Greek geek, the grammatical form is a periphrastic
imperfect). Without commitment, any corporate prayer ini-
tiative will die faster than a New Year resolution about diet.

Church leaders, in particular, need the virtue of sanctified stubbornness. We will face people voting "no" with feet

and wallets. We must kill our egos and kindle conviction.

Pastor Jim Cymbala does not shy from facing the core issue. He boldly calls others to face the facts.

> Pastors and churches have to get uncomfortable enough to say, 'We are not New Testament Christians if we don't have a prayer life.' This conviction makes us squirm a little, but how else will there be a breakthrough with God? If we truly think about what Acts 2:42 says – 'They devoted themselves to the apostles' teaching and to the fellowship, to the breaking of bread and to prayer' – we can see that prayer is almost a proof of a church's normalcy. Calling on the name of the Lord is the fourth great hallmark in the list. If my church or your church isn't praying, we shouldn't be boasting in our orthodoxy or Sunday morning attendance figures.[4]

He has seen big numbers, but they have not blinded him to the priority of prayer.

Be Creative

The third step is to be creative. I can imagine fellow pastors thinking, "How do we do this? Give us practical advice. Theory is not enough."

I will do that in tomorrow's reading. For now, I make one plea: employ the same level of energy and creativity you have already used in designing programs, handling facility challenges, doing strategic planning, and casting vision. Multi-year plans are common in ministry. Create a plan to gradually implement and increase corporate prayer.

The task will be hardest in large churches. I led a very large church and know the challenges. James 4:10 remains true. "Humble yourselves before the Lord, and he will lift you up." Let him lift you, and he will help you do the heavy lifting.

We must all wait on the Lord as the early church did. It is a big mistake for a church to be program-heavy but *lite-wait*. To do the heavy lifting we must join the *heavy-wait* class. James 1:5 says, "If any of you lacks wisdom, you should ask God, who gives generously to all without finding fault, and it will be given to you."

Ask God to help us take these three steps forward...and no steps back.

THESE THINGS CAN WORK

The ignition key stuck in the tumbler. The engine cut off, but the key would not come loose. Wiggling the key proved worthless. A costly trip to the dealership seemed inevitable.

Then I had an epiphany – YouTube! Punch in a problem, and someone shows how to solve it. A regular Joe displayed a fix for my car that was so simple I doubted him. Locate a plastic ring on the shaft near the shifter grip. Slide the ring up a bit and you solve the problem. So he said.

His solution seemed crazy. The ring was not even close to the steering column. Because the proposed fix cost nothing, I tried it. It worked like a charm.

Corporate prayer need not be a complex production. At heart, corporate prayer is God's saints (all saved sinners) talking to him. Some prayer books offer good, practical suggestions for organizing and leading group prayer. Some advice, however, seems overly complex. I will share simple things that have worked in congregations I have served.

Regular Sunday worship services

The idea of taking, say, 20 minutes for corporate prayer in worship services astonishes people. Spending 20 minutes singing and listening to special music in a worship service fails to astonish anyone. Why the divergent responses? Remember that corporate prayer is music to God's ears.

One way to include corporate prayer in services is through groups formed on the spot. This worked well for us even in a sanctuary with pews. Encourage people to move around week by week so they do not always pray with the same people. Ask them to start praying as quickly as they reasonably can. Signal the time to close by playing a soft instrumental. The person praying at that time is the final one.

Before we formed these prayer groups, I briefly explained to visitors each time why we did it. I told them that no one in any group would be forced to pray. I gave them the option of sitting alone and praying quietly.

Sometimes just one group led the congregation in prayer from the platform. The prayer circle could be just elders, other leaders, or a mix of members. We arranged the day's group in advance. They knew they were there to lead the body, not to perform, covertly preach, or enjoy a personal prayer session. Microphones help in large rooms.

Liturgical prayer can work well with these group

approaches. It has a long pedigree for good reason. When done intentionally, liturgical prayer reinforces the unity of the church. Consider how it might deepen the united prayer life of your congregation.

Align these approaches with various seasons in the church. Vary the approach in different types of services, and pray at different points in services. The leaders must forge links between the life of the church and the best forms.

Regular prayer meetings

We took a clean, direct approach. A prayer sheet helped guide prayer. It had three sections.

The first section was "A Priority Prayer." We printed a prayer directly from the Bible. People incorporated the themes in the session. Centering on the word of God kept the meeting from degenerating into an organ recital ("pray for my gall bladder and my uncle's kidneys").

The next section was "Praise and Thanks." It focused on God's glories and the good things he does.

The last section was "Requests." We kept the items up to date. They included important aspects of church life, missions, civic leaders, and even an occasional gall bladder.

People would share prayer requests at the beginning of the meeting, but we kept that part brief. The prayer sheets were available online and in the church foyer for those unable to make a given meeting. This minimalist approach made it easier to enlist prayer meeting leaders. We maintained consistency and maximized prayer time.

It might surprise some, but having music at prayer meetings made no observable difference in the quality of prayer. Music does not create worship; music expresses worship. Worship is a response to God that can include music, but singing is not mandatory at prayer meetings. Some of the most God-centered prayer meetings had no singing. We did not feature music at most regular prayer meetings. Meetings were easier to arrange, especially with multiple weekly prayer meetings.

We also did not feature Bible lessons and devotionals. We simply read that week's "Priority Prayer" from Scripture. Many "prayer meetings" are Bible studies with minimal prayer tagged onto the end. We taught the Bible in many other venues. Prayer meetings focused on prayer. Typically we spent 75% of the meeting praying.

Slots for the meetings varied. We usually held one midweek meeting and one on Sunday morning. We encouraged people to come regularly but urged participation at least a few times a quarter.

Special prayer services

We held prayer services for National Day of Prayer, 9/11 Memorials, interchurch ministry, strategic initiatives, and for the persecuted church. These longer meetings included music (instrumental and singing), a meditation from Scripture, and testimonies.

The best approach combined small group prayer with prayer led from the platform. At times we dismissed the people from the main auditorium to various rooms, thereby creating multiple prayer meetings. I called people back to the main room by playing the bugle call Assembly on my trumpet. Perhaps your lips are not up to that approach. Other means can do the job.

Additional Thoughts

Teach regularly about prayer from God's word to make all the above approaches fruitful. People need to know why corporate prayer is important, and how it fits into church life. Literature, on-screen displays, verbal direction by leaders, newcomer classes, and personal conversations help orient people to communal prayer.

Use sentence prayers for a portion of the prayer session. For example, encourage people to finish the sentence "I praise you Lord for…." These sentence starters draw children into vocal prayer and encourage quiet people to speak. Maintain sentence prayers while adding longer prayers into the mix.

Remind people that prayer is a family conversation with the best parent of all. Prayer is not public speaking. I have offered a free funeral to anyone who prays out loud for the first time and keels over because of it! No one ever needed to take that deal.

In multi-lingual meetings special guidance promotes

understanding. A church plant I supported prayed in both English and Spanish. A friend told me how hearing people pray in another language was especially encouraging. When she stretched to pray in halting Spanish, she brought tears (of joy, not laughter) to the eyes of Hispanic brothers and sisters. The leaders did not translate everything, but they worked hard to make the experience meaningful to all.

Sealed with a KISS

The KISS approach to corporate prayer seems best to me – Keep It Simple, Saints. Some of the tactics above might seem too simple, but they have worked well in congregations with very different dynamics. As they say in commercials, your results may vary. Implementation will probably try your patience, but these tactics are worth a good try.

EIGHT KINDS OF PRAY-ERS

Books galore break prayers into types. I will now break pray-ers (the people praying) into types. Oddly enough, I divide types to coach about united prayer.

Newbies

People who are new to corporate prayer don't know what to expect, so explain some basics. There is no special vocabulary, approved tone of voice, required emotional state, minimum length of prayer, or set attendance standard. The goal is for people to come as regularly as they can, pray naturally, and use plain words. No one expects King James English (though thou might hearest some faithful people doeth that by long practice). God loves prayers that are honorable and sincere, even if those prayers are not as smooth as fine stained glass.

Enthusiasts

If you are enthusiastic about praying, beware of a danger arising from that blessed state. You can harm corporate prayer if you do not curb your enthusiasm. Pray long and often in private prayer, but in a body-oriented prayer meeting, all should have opportunity. Pray a few times and do not go long. Paul told the early church that "the spirits of the prophets are subject to the control of the prophets" (1Cor 14:32). If those enthusiasts could limit themselves for the good of the body, all can.

Be especially careful during silence. A less experienced person might be getting up the courage to pray out loud. Even the praying in heaven pauses for silence (Rev 8:1-10). We can welcome some quiet in our lives. Dead air is bad for radio; some stillness is good in prayer meetings.

Scaredy Cats

Some people fear they will be forced (or at least pressured) into praying out loud. Don't do that to anyone. Even though I am not afraid to pray out loud, I have sat silently at many prayer meetings, nourished by the prayers. I already said that I plead with habitually silent ones to reconsider their approach. I encourage them to break the sound barrier (Bell X-1 pilot Chuck Yeager should not have all the fun).

The Wanderers

I fit this group. My mind wanders at prayer meetings. I am blessed and burdened by a very active cranium. When my mind wanders, the Great Shepherd brings it back to green pastures and still waters. We wanderers have a lot of company and a patient guide. Think about that. If your attention just wandered, think about it again.

The Wild Ones

People sometimes do inappropriate things at prayer meetings. Don't turn a prayer session into a platform for partisan politics. Don't preach under the disguise of prayer. Don't gossip. Leaders must deal with these problems directly but delicately. But members of the body should not sit on the sidelines and leave all to leaders. The best people to calm the wild ones are those closest to them.

Seniors

I mean the seasoned citizens. Our culture idolizes youthfulness, but the church family needs to hear grace-seasoned hearts. Seniors count. Some have hearing problems and can't catch every word, but their presence speaks volumes. All participants should speak loudly enough to help seniors hear the prayers.

Children and Youth

Younger people bring energy and fresh perspective older people need. Pastors should encourage whole families to take part. Parents should use good judgment if a baby gets fussy, or if a child needs special attention. Leave the meeting to settle things and then return. I doubt that an early church prayer session was as placid as a library reading room.

An unlikely prayer duo formed one of my fondest ministry memories. A senior citizen and a seven-year-old sat next to one another at a prayer meeting. They were not related except through the gospel. Both prayed out loud. Each benefited from the other, and both benefited all of us. We can make such memories everywhere.

Cross-demographic prayer uniquely builds the fellowship. I have received formal training in two small group systems. My wife and I have hosted small groups in our home. I have provided standard small groups for many people. Good things came from those ministries, but I have never seen bonds of love and service as strong as those formed in cross-demographic prayer meetings.

Busy People

This group includes almost everybody. My friend told me that the greatest miracle of the day can be when God parts the Red Sea of schedule so her family can get to a prayer meeting. Jesus did various miracles, but he never made more minutes in his day. We can triumph over time challenges and distractions the same way he did – by making time the hard way.

Body Beautiful

Many people fit more than one of the above categories, and people change categories over time. I have been in almost every one of them. Diversity in unity makes the body beautiful. Perhaps you know the following insult joke. "How can you quickly lose ten pounds of ugly fat? Cut off your head." When we cut the body apart and from our exalted Head in prayer, we all lose.

Whether you sit in a folding chair, stand, or take a knee or two – be the body, pray, and produce real beauty. Every type can appreciate that.

PART FIVE

PERSONAL PLOTTING

We draw toward the end of our reading journey. This last part of the book prods you to plot a course for your response. Reading is one thing; acting is another matter. Apply what we have seen from Scripture and we will, by grace, improve the prayer life of the church. What a great prospect and privilege!

THINGS NO BOOK CAN DO

have played trumpet for many years. I did not read a book, pick up a trumpet, and play a 12-bar blues, a march, or a concerto. I had to listen to other players, try playing, and sound clumsy at times. I had to put my need to grow above my ego. I had to persevere.

I read a lot of books and wrote one. But there are limits to what a book can do. My trumpet teachers used books as helpful tools, but without playing I could not have become a trumpeter.

You cannot learn to pray by reading books, including mine. You must listen to others, pray with them, and sound clumsy at times. You must put your need to grow above your ego. You must persevere.

Megan Hill points the way.

I can think of no better – or simpler – discipleship program than for more mature and less mature believers to sit diligently under the preaching of the word and then to pray together. I can also think of nothing more exciting. This was how you first learned the faith, this was how the members of the early church grew (Acts 2:42), this was how Christ is even now conforming to himself the saints in Korea and the saints in my own church, and it is how those around you will come to maturity too. Brothers and sisters, are you ready?[1]

You learn to pray with the body by praying with the body. That is God's plan.

Jesus is the only sinless human in history. He alone has power over life and death. Even he did not pray only by himself. The one who saves people prayed with people.

I have been playing trumpet for over five decades. I still listen to others, play with others, and sound clumsy at times. It is the same with praying corporately. I still listen to others, pray with others, and sound clumsy at times. Join me.

Whenever I played trumpet, my dad said it sounded great – even the clumsy parts. He is with the Lord now and (presumably) cannot hear me play today. When we pray together in the Spirit, it sounds great to our Father – even the clumsy parts. He can always hear us pray. He loves to hear the whole ensemble.

Please him. Play your part.

WHAT WILL YOU MAKE OF IT?

My book is almost done. The real ending is up to you. What will you do with what I have written? I hope you will judge it all by Scripture. The prime question is: "What will we all do with what God's perfect book says about the church and prayer?"

Start with self-examination. Do you have "an obedience" for prayer? If so, seek outlets to express that passion corporately. If not, repent. Everyone must trust and obey. There is no other way.

If you are in seminary, consider highlighting prayer in your studies. Much exegetical work remains to be done. Study culture and how it helps or hinders prayer. Do not wait until you are a pastor to pray with the body. Do it *now*.

If you are a church leader, how will you introduce or fortify corporate prayer among the people for whom you are responsible? How will you teach and preach about prayer in the future? At what speed will you proceed to be prudent but not tentative? What part will corporate prayer play in strategic planning or vision casting? What are you willing to risk for prayer to blossom in the body?

If you are a church member, how will you introduce or fortify prayer among the fellowship? Consider talking to your pastor about prayer in the body. Be respectful and patient. My goal is *not* to breed crazed prayer terriers nipping at pastoral heels. If you introduce this book to a church leader, say that it comes from a pastor who has made his share of mistakes. Don't talk to your pastor *about* prayer unless you are already talking to God *for* your pastor. Please reread the preceding sentence two more times.

If you are a parent, how will you introduce your children to corporate prayer? If they already take part, how can you build on what you have begun?

Whether a church is humming along, is plodding, or is in crisis, corporate prayer remains essential. I have seen churches go through trying times, but not turn to corporate prayer. They sought solutions for a faltering ministry in consultants, an interim pastor, a new pastor, a vision statement, the latest seminar, and exciting programs, but failed to gather in earnest for prayer.

Embrace true success. Make prayer a priority in every season.

How well does your church accept the Lord's invitation from his throne of grace? How often do you ask the helper to purge his church of contaminants like individualism, pragmatism, and consumerism? How earnestly do you seek his mercies for all we need?

To borrow a line from poet Stephen Vincent Benét, we must stop living "in vast indifference at so many gifts unsought."[1] We need to change our ways and pray to the one who never changes. Hebrews 13:6-8 tells the church, "Therefore, we may boldly say, 'The Lord is my helper; I will not be afraid. What can man do to me?' Remember your leaders who have spoken God's word to you. As you carefully observe the outcome of their lives, imitate their faith. Jesus Christ is the same yesterday, today, and forever." We can always count on Jesus.

I may not be your leader, but I have given you the word of God. Listening carefully to the Bible about corporate prayer (and what it says about many other things) has changed my life and my approach to ministry. I heard the word and I grew.

Do you hear what I hear? If not, *why* not? If so, what *will* you do?

The real corporate prayer challenge is *not* a 30-day reading program. A kickstart is just a start. A motorcycle must maintain momentum to go places. The real challenge for us all is to submit to God's word about prayer and maintain pace over the *long* run.

Run, church, run! Go to the throne of grace, and never stop.

FARE WELL MY FRIENDS

The theater audience had taken a strange journey. At the end of the play, a peculiar creature made a plea.

If we shadows have offended,
Think but this, and all is mended,
That you have but slumber'd here
While these visions did appear.
And this weak and idle theme,
No more yielding but a dream.[1]

Puck bids farewell to his audience with those words at the end of "A Midsummer Night's Dream" by William Shakespeare.

As I bid my book audience goodbye, I may have offended some. But my closing appeal is the *opposite* of Puck's council. I write as one who took too long to become "woke" to corporate prayer. I don't mind disturbing the similar slumber of others so they can thrive. Corporate prayer is no "weak and idle theme." It is a *vital* theme. We are weak, but God is strong. We are shadows, but Jesus is sovereign. If we pray well in his name, we will fare well indeed.

Listen to a far better man and author than me or the Bard. The Apostle Paul wrote to a church he loved saying, "Get up, sleeper, and rise up from the dead, and Christ will shine on you. Pay careful attention, then, to how you live – not as unwise people but as wise – making the most of the time, because the days are evil. So don't be foolish, but understand what the Lord's will is" (Eph 5:14b-17).

I close with Jesus, an infinitely better man than Paul. The Lord sounded the same call to a church he loved. "Wake up! Strengthen what remains and is about to die, for I have not found your deeds complete in the sight of my God." (Rev 3:2). We must be dreaming if we think Jesus is completely pleased with the prayer life of his church in America. We need to toss off the comfy covers and get down to business.

All can be mended. The Lord is still gracious. The body just needs to repent, get up, and get back to corporate prayer.

Do that, and fare well my friends.

APPENDIX

Church leaders and scholars from a variety of church traditions recognize that Acts 2:42 serves as a fundamental model for church life. I have not found any writings that say the verse is only descriptive. The following quotes are all about Acts 2:42 in context and represent a modest portion of my research findings.

"Wherever these things take place, there certainly the Holy Spirit cannot long be excluded, but rather he will soon arrive with all his goods, mercies and gifts, temporal and eternal. So help us God!" Johann Spangenberg, "Die Apostel Geschichte," in Acts: *Reformation Commentary on Scripture*, vol. 6 (Downers Grove: IVP, 2014), 36. Written in 1544.

"Luke is listing the items in which the church engaged. He shows four characteristics by which the true church can be judged. Do we look for the true church of Christ? It is pictured here." *John Calvin, Acts*, ed. Alister McGrath and

J. I. Packer (Wheaton: Crossway, 1995), 48. Written in 1552.

"And those converts who were baptized, not only believed the same things, but they also believed in the practice of the same duties which the apostles observed; for it is said, that they continued with them *steadfastly*, in the *breaking of bread* and in *prayers*, as well as in *doctrine*." Cyprian Strong, A *Discourse on Acts ii.* 42 (London: Forgotten Books, 2017), 4. Written in 1791.

"With a few touches it describes the mode of life in the most ancient Christian church, and exhibits the earliest elements of worship. The peculiar spirit of the gospel is exhibited by this description quite clearly before our eyes." Hermann Olshusen, *Biblical Commentary on the New Testament* (New York: Sheldon, Blakeman & Co, 1858), 212.

"These are, indeed, the four essential elements of all true Christian association." Melanchthon W. Jacobus, *Notes Critical and Explanatory on the Acts of the Apostles* (Philadelphia: Presbyterian Board of Publication, 1859), 83.

"Vss. 42-47: Here we have a picture of the infant church in which the idea of a church is realized to a very high degree and which is evidently portrayed here, to point out the essential character of the church." J.B. Lightfoot, *The Acts of the Apostles: A Newly Discovered Commentary* (Downers Grove: IVP, 2014), 90-91. Compiled from handwritten teaching notes Lightfoot produced in the second half of the 1800s.

"Let it not be for nothing that these plain common words have been now spoken upon the Christian life of the first days of the Gospel. We have gone almost as far (such must be our reflections) from a primitive piety as from an original righteousness. The Gospel salt has indeed lost its savour: who shall season it? Apostolical teaching, Christian fellowship, holy Communion, public prayers, all are neglected; in comparison at least with the Scripture model, in comparison at least with the practice of the saints." C. J. Vaughn, *Lectures on the Acts of the Apostles* (London: Macmillan, 1890), 50.

"Membership in this society meant a continuous effort: it was a *persevering adherence*, both (a) to persons and (b) to duties, especially prayer. Here S. Luke gives us the four essentials that must not be abandoned." Richard Belward Rackham, *The Acts of the Apostles* (London: Methuen,1901), 33.

"In these words are set forth the characteristic marks of the new Christian life to which the converts of Pentecost were pledged by their Baptism." James Hastings, *The Great Texts of the Bible: Acts and Romans* (Edinburgh: T&T Clark, 1911), 47.

"These are four ordinances of Christian fellowship. Baptism is not an ordinance of Christian fellowship; it is the ordinance that indicates the entrance upon fellowship. The four ordinances to be constantly observed in Christian fellowship are: the apostles' teaching, the fellowship, the breaking of bread, and the prayers." G. Campbell Morgan, *The Acts of the Apostles* (New York: Fleming H. Revell Company, 1924), 92.

"In the book of Acts (2:42, 46; 20:7) instruction, preaching, prayer and breaking of bread are mentioned, and mentioned in such a way as clearly to show that these elements were, from the beginning, the foundation of all the worship life of the Christian community." Oscar Cullmann, *Early Christian Worship* (Louisville: Westminster Press, 1978), 12. Written in 1950.

"The church has drifted far from the simplicity of worship of the Early Church. Did not the Spirit inspire those first disciples to set forth a pattern of worship for all ages? Teaching of doctrine, fellowship around the Word, the breaking of bread, intercession – these were powerfully influential in the lives of the early saints. And their 'togetherness' made an impact upon the world all around." Herbert Lockyer, *All the Prayers of the Bible* (Grand Rapids: Zondervan, 1959), 230.

"Prayer is the inevitable conclusion of true doctrine. The first Christians started with the apostles' teaching, and that led to prayer." Martyn Lloyd-Jones, *Authentic Christianity* (Wheaton: Crossway, 2000), 162. Written in 1965.

"Prayer is the best test of an individual, and it is also the best test of a church. A church can be flourishing, she can be successful in terms of organizations, she can be tremendously active and appear to be prosperous; but if you want to know whether she is a real church or not, examine the amount of prayer that takes place. Prayer is the inevitable conclusion of true doctrine. The first Christians started with the apostle's teaching, and that led to prayer." Martyn Lloyd-Jones, *Authentic Christianity* (Wheaton: Crossway, 2000), 162.

"That which was so vital to the experience of the individual was also a part of the life of the church as believers joined together in united prayer. They 'continued steadfastly … in prayers.' (Ac 2:42), whether in homes (2:46) or in the temple (3:1). Exhortations and instruction for prayers enjoined in the epistles were certainly meant for the assembled believers as well as for individuals (Eph 6:18; Phil 4:6; Col 4:2; 1 Th 5:17; 1 Ti 2:1-2, 8)." Robert L. Saucy, *The Church in God's Program* (Chicago: Moody Press, 1972), 182.

"No doubt Luke intends us to recognize that verses 42-47 describe what happens to people in whom the Holy Spirit dwells. Here is the ideal, to which the later church must always look for an exemplar." Anthony Lee Ash, *The Acts of the Apostles: Part 1* (Hurst: Sweet, 1979), 57.

"Here are the four essential elements in the religious practice of the Christian Church." I. Howard Marshall, *The Acts of the Apostles* (Grand Rapids: Wm. Eerdmans, 1980), 83.

"Four basic characteristics must be present in the church in every age. 'And they devoted themselves' marks the perennial issue of every Christian community." Gerhard A. Krodel, *Acts* (Minneapolis: Augsburg Fortress, 1986), 92.

"How can you identify a real church? Notice the four marks of identification." J. Vernon McGee, *Acts: Chapters 1-14* (Nashville: Nelson, 1991), 40.

"Acts 2:42 delineates the basic ingredients of church life: 'They were continually devoting themselves to the apostles' teaching and to fellowship, to the breaking of bread (Communion) and to prayer.' They had all the ingredients they needed to have a functioning, God-blessed,

Spirit-directed church." John MacArthur, *The Master's Plan for the Church* (Chicago: Moody Press, 1991), 87.

"We find in these practices of the early church – devoted to the apostles' teaching, fellowship, breaking of bread, and prayer – the four essential elements in the religious practice of the Christian church. The early church built on the life of faith that had been developed in their Jewish practices, but discipleship to the risen Jesus gave a distinctive flavor to this spiritual life. We see here the essential ingredients of the way in which the new community sustained their life of discipleship." Michael J. Wilkins, *Following the Master: A Biblical Theology of Discipleship* (Grand Rapids: Zondervan, 1992), 277-78.

"The Church was established and normal church life began. The first biblical description of what New Testament Christians do in church is given in the second chapter of Acts. 'And they continued steadfastly in the apostle's doctrine and fellowship, in the breaking of bread, and *in prayers* (Acts 2:42, emphasis mine). Corporate prayer was not peripheral back then as it often is now. It was central." C. Peter Wagner, *Churches that Pray* (Ventura: Regal Books, 1993), 107.

"The measure of a church's success is about enhancing truth in the midst of a non-truth culture; community involvement and fellowship in a culture that resists commitment to others and celebrates privatism and isolation; the celebration of history in our rootedness in the Cross, pictured at the Lord's Table in a world that has little time for or interest in the implications of history on our present lives. And it continues in prayer in a society that cele-brates self-sufficiency." Joseph M. Stowell, *Shepherding the Church: Effective Spiritual Leadership in a Changing Culture* (Chicago: Moody Press, 1994), 87.

"Those elements are the unique expressions of the life of the church. They are the means of grace by which the church becomes what God wants it to be." John MacArthur, Acts 1-12 (Chicago: Moody Press, 1994), 85.

"Obviously this description is intended as an example for us and our assemblies." James Montgomery Boice, Acts: *An Expositional Commentary* (Grand Rapids: Baker Book House, 1997), 55.

"This passage gives us a picture of early Christian com-munity life. Each of the things the new Christians practiced are given often in the Scriptures, especially in the New Testament letters, as essential aspects of Christian living." Ajith Fernando, Acts: *The NIV Application Commentary* (Grand Rapids: Zondervan, 1998), 125.

"At various times in Acts, especially in the early chap-ters, Luke gives summary reports of how the church is doing. Here we have the first. In it our author describes what a biblical church really looks like, not only in the first century, but in every century from the Lord's ascension until his second coming." Kenneth Gangel, Acts: *Holman New Testament Commentary* (Nashville: Holman, 1998), 31.

"What they are described as doing is so obvious that if Luke had not written it one would have conjectured it. Faithful adherence to the Christian way was what Luke meant to describe and by implication to commend." C. K.

Barrett, Acts (Edinburgh: T&T Clark, 2002), 34.

"The interrelation between these four criteria, and particularly between the first two (defined in modern ecumenical usage as 'faith and order;' 6:2-4), would dominate all subsequent efforts to understand the unity of the church and the divisions within Christendom, as well as the efforts to obey the imperative of Christ's prayer 'that they may all be one' (John 17:21)." Jaroslav Pelikan, Acts (Grand Rapids: Brazos, 2005), 60.

"Verse 42 is regularly cited as the earliest description of four central elements in Christian worship, which should characterize the church as it gathers in any time and place: preaching or teaching God's word, fellowship, the Lord's Supper (Communion or the Eucharist), and prayer." Craig L. Blomberg, From Pentecost to Patmos: An Introduction to Acts through Revelation (Nashville: B&H, 2006), 28.

"Verses 42-47 present a Lukan summary of the newly restored faith community. This particular summary offers an ideal portrait of early Christian life. Verse 42 introduces features of such communal life upon which vv. 43-47 elaborate." J. Bradley Chance, Acts: Smyth & Helwys Bible Commentary (Macon: Smyth & Helwys, 2007), 59.

"When we look to the early church members' own practice, we see that they 'devoted themselves to the apostles' teaching and to the fellowship, to the breaking of bread and to prayer' (Acts 2:42). In other words, the early Christians were devoted to hearing the Word of God (the apostles' teaching) in the fellowship of believers, to the Lord's Supper (the sacraments), and to prayer. The Lord has not changed – he uses these means of grace today to sanctify his people." Kate Treick, "Simple Grace, Simple Growth," *Modern Reformation* (March/April 2009): 25.

"The combined working of these four factors produces the very fabric and structure in which the priesthood of all believers is called to function. Acts 2:42 presents the irreducible minimum of what constitutes the operation of a New Testament church." Sam Thorpe Jr., *No Other Foundation: An Exposition of Acts 2:42* (Dubuque: ECS Ministries, 2010), 54.

"In all these activities of teaching, fellowship and sharing, breaking of bread, and praying we see a well-rounded picture of the church, the marks of authentic embodiment of the Sprit in the community's life, a canon for the measurement of the church's activity today." William Willimon, *Acts: A Bible Commentary for Teaching and Preaching* (Louisville: Westminster John Knox Press, 2010), 41.

"The primary worship passage in Acts is 2:42-47, and in verse 42 Luke provides the 'four pillars' of the earliest worship – teaching, fellowship, the breaking of bread, and prayer. It says the believers 'devoted themselves' to these things, a critical concept in Acts (1:14; 2:42, 46; 6:4; 8:13; 10:7) that stresses both unity in pursuit of a goal and serious persistence in attaining these things." Grant Osborne, "Moving Forward on Our Knees: Corporate Prayer in the New Testament," *Journal of the Evangelical Theological Society* (June 2010), 254.

"Throughout the book of Acts, the growth of the church – its mission – is identified by the phrase, 'And the word of God spread.' The regular gathering of the saints for 'the apostles' teaching and the fellowship,' 'the breaking of bread,' and 'the prayers' (Ac 2:42) is not treated in Acts merely as an exercise in spiritual togetherness but as itself the sign that the kingdom had arrived in the Spirit. Furthermore, it issued in a community that brought wonder and awe to its neighbors." Michael Horton, *The Christian Faith: A Systematic Theology for Pilgrims on the Way* (Grand Rapids: Zondervan, 2011), 899.

"Though praying together is not elevated above the devotion to the apostles' teaching, the fellowship, and the breaking of bread, it is accorded the same level of importance as the other three foundational commitments new believers make." Andy Chambers, *Exemplary Life: A Theology of Church Life in Acts* (Nashville: B&H, 2012), 70.

"Here are the rudiments of Christian worship, though Luke did not elaborate. From these we may structure for ourselves an order of service for Sunday morning. These four elements give us four essential activities." David F. Wells, *God in the Whirlwind: How the Holy-Love of God Reorients Our World* (Wheaton: Crossway, 2014), 204.

"This summary is one of the few places where Luke tells us what happens after people are converted, and it emphasizes key elements of the church's life." David E. Garland, *Acts* (Grand Rapids: Baker Book House, 2017), 33.

MANY THANKS

I thank God for the people who modeled prayer for me, taught me the basics, and encouraged me to pray. I am grateful to those who prayed for me and with me. Many people have allowed me to shepherd them into corporate prayer. Nothing church members have done has encouraged me more.

I thank God for making me a pastor. Even considering the pain and challenges, I have known much joy in the work. My original plans were to be an architect or a professional musician. I am glad God had other plans for me.

I thank God for helping me hold the course in the face of congregational and pastoral pushback against corporate prayer. My family and I have paid a price for following the core convictions in this book. I am not naturally courageous. Most of my life I was prone to please people as a defense mechanism against disapproval. Praise God for training me out of that mode. He enrolled me in the college of hard knocks, and he saw me through to graduation. He is still schooling me about faithfulness under pressure.

I am grateful for all who encouraged me to write this book. I especially thank the C242 family whose support is precious. Jess Rainer provided helpful guidance and resources. My manuscript readers improved the book in countless ways: David Bush, Natalie Bush, Francine Lawler, Jonathan Lawler, Ellen Schmidt, Mark Schmidt, Becky Ward, and Christine Yalanis. Jacey Lawler did tons of tedious formatting. Beth Morgan merits special thanks for her editing and support. I owe them all, but I own any mistakes that remain in the text.

I thank God for my nuclear family. My wife Francine is a paragon of prayer. My son Jonathan and daughter Jacey walk the talk in this book. Pardon the pun, but our family is the bomb! Our extended family is dynamite too.

Finally, thank you for taking this reading journey.

Soli Deo Gloria.

Preface – A Challenge

1. P. T. Forsyth, *The Soul of Prayer* (London: Charles H. Kelly, 1916), 9.
2. George Orwell, *Why I Write* (New York: Penguin Books, 2005), 1.
3. Helmut Thielicke, preface to *The Trouble with the Church: A Call For Renewal*, ed. and trans. John W. Doberstein (Grand Rapids: Baker Book House, 1978), XV-XVI.

Day Three – A Rare One for the Books

1. Edward McKendree Bounds, *Preacher and Prayer* (Breinigsville: Kessinger, 2010), 123.

Day Five – The Last Thing the Church Wants to Do

1. For an overview, see *Teach Us to Pray: Prayer in the Bible and the World*, ed. D. A. Carson (Eugene: Wipf and Stock Publishers, 2002).

2. Sinclair Ferguson, *The Grace of Repentance* (Wheaton: Crossway, 2010), 55.
3. Bounds, 36.

Day Six – The Last Thing I Intended

1. Ray Bradbury, *The Stories of Ray Bradbury* (New York: Knopf, 1986), 290.
2. William Cowper, *Cowper: Verse and Letters*, ed. Brian Spiller (Cambridge: Harvard University Press, 1968), 154.

Day Seven – Two Problems

1. Daniel Henderson and Margaret Saylar, *Fresh Encounters: Experiencing Transformation Through United Worship-Based Prayer* (Carol Stream: NavPress, 2008), 43.
2. Daniel T. Jenkins, "Prayer and the Service of God," in *Journal of Theological Studies* 45, (July/October 1944): 88.
3. Trevin K. Wax, *Eschatological Discipleship: Leading Christians to Understand Their Historical and Cultural Context* (Nashville: B&H Academic, 2018), 170-1.
4. Michael J. Weiss, *The Clustered World: How We Live, What We Buy, and What It All Means About Who We Are* (Boston: Little, Brown, 2000), 12-13.
5. Weiss, 10.
6. Zach Schlegel, "Corporate Prayer Is More than Your Personal Quiet Time," *9Marks Journal*, (June 21, 2016),

accessed December 12, 2019, https://www.9marks. org/article/corporate-prayer-is-more-than-your- personal- quiet-time/.

Day Eight – The Things People Say

1. Charles Spurgeon, "A Call to Worship," in *The Metropolitan Tabernacle Pulpit: Sermons Preached and Revised*, vol. 19 (Pasadena: Pilgrim Publication, 1981), 218.
2. John Calvin, *Institutes of the Christian Religion*, ed. John T. McNeill, trans. Ford Lewis Battles (Philadelphia: Westminster Press, 1960), 3.20.29, 892.
3. George Herbert, *The Temple*, ed. Henry L. Carrigan Jr., (Brewster: Paraclete Press, 2001), 18.
4. G. K. Chesterton, *What's Wrong with the World?* (London: Cassell, 1912), 39.
5. Henry Grattan Guinness, *The Revival in Ireland: Letters from Ministers and Medical Men in Ulster on the Revival of Religion in the North of Ireland Addressed to the Rev. H. Grattan Guinness* (Lexington: ULAN Press, 2013), 8-9.

Day Nine – Things That Temporarily Shut My Mouth

1. David F. Wells, *God in the Whirlwind: How the Holy-Love of God Reorients Our World* (Wheaton: Crossway, 2014), 204-5.

2. William Willimon, Acts: A *Bible Commentary for Preaching and Teaching* (Louisville: Westminster John Knox Press, 2010), 40.

Part Three Introduction

1. Sara Groves, "The Word," INO Records, track 2 on *Conversations*, 2001, compact disc.

Day Ten – The Problem with Two or Three

1. Craig L. Blomberg, *The New American Commentary*, vol. 22, *Matthew* (Nashville: B&H, 1992), 280-1.

Day Eleven – Thing 1 and Thing 2

1. Dr. Seuss, *The Cat in the Hat* (New York: Random House, 1957), 1-2.

Day Twelve – The Remaining Issue

1. Joyce Kilmer, "Trees," in *The Best Loved Poems of the American People*, ed. Hazel Felleman (New York: Doubleday, 1936), 561.

Day Fourteen – The First Four Things

1. Richard John Neuhaus, *Freedom for Ministry* (Grand Rapids: Wm. Eerdmans, 1992), 33.
2. R. C. H. Lenski, *Commentary on the New Testament: The Interpretation of the Acts of the Apostles* (Peabody: Hendrickson Publishers, 2001), 117.
3. Grant Osborne, "Moving Forward on Our Knees: Corporate Prayer in the New Testament," *Journal of the Evangelical Theological Society*, (June 2010): 253.
4. John Calvin, Acts, ed. Alister McGrath and J. I. Packer, (Wheaton: Crossway, 1995), 48.

Day Fifteen – Time to Be the Temple

1. D. A. Carson, *The Cross and Christian Ministry: An Exposition of Passages from 1 Corinthians* (Grand Rapids: Baker Book House, 1993), 83-84.

Day Eighteen – Prayer and the Worship Leader

1. Curtis C. Mitchell, *Praying Jesus' Way: A New Approach to Personal Prayer* (Old Tappan: Fleming H. Revell Company, 1977), 123.

Day Twenty – The Big Bully

1. C. S. Lewis, *Screwtape Letters* (New York: Macmillan, 1961), 21.
2. T. W. Rolleston, preface to *The Teaching of Epictetus* (New York: Columbian Publishing Company, 1891), XXIX.
3. Charles Spurgeon, *The Salt-Cellars: A Collection of Proverbs and Quaint Sayings*, vol. 1, (Pasadena: Pilgrim Publications, 1975), 58.

Day Twenty-One – This Thing Does Not Work

1. S. D. Gordon, *Quiet Talks on Prayer* (New York: Fleming H. Revell Company, 1904), 16.

Day Twenty-Two – To Buy or Not to Buy?

1. Ferguson, 39.

Day Twenty-Three – An Important Thing Church Leaders Don't Want to Do, But Must

1. William Willimon, "Preaching in An Age That Has Lost Its Moral Compass," in *Exilic Preaching: Testimony for Christian Exiles in an Increasingly Hostile Culture*, ed.

Erskine Clarke (Harrisburg: Trinity Press International, 1998), 121-22.

2. Abraham Lincoln, *The Life and Writings of Abraham Lincoln*, ed. Philip Van Doren Stern (New York: Modern Library, 2000), 843.

3. Christina Rosetti, *The Complete Poems* (New York: Penguin Books, 2001), 251.

Day Twenty-Five – Three Steps Forward

1. The Beach Boys, "Sloop John B," Capitol Records, track 7 on *Pet Sounds*, 1966, compact disc.

2. A. W. Tozer, *The Pursuit of God* (Camp Hill: Christian Publications, 1982), 17.

3. A. W. Tozer, *Voice of a Prophet: Who Speaks for God?* ed. James L. Snyder (Minneapolis: Bethany House, 2014), 23.

4. Jim Cymbala and Dean Merrill, *Fresh Wind, Fresh Fire: What Happens When God's Spirit Invades the Heart of His People* (Grand Rapids: Zondervan, 1997), 51.

Day Twenty-Eight – Things No Book Can Do

1. Megan Hill, *Praying Together: The Priority and Privileges of Prayer in Our Homes, Communities, and Churches* (Wheaton: Crossway, 2016), 80.

Day Twenty-Nine – What Will You Make of It?

1. Stephen Vincent Benét, *John Brown's Body* (New York: Holt, Rinehard, and Winston, 1968), 8.

Day Thirty – Fare Well My Friends

1. William Shakespeare, A *Midsummer Night's Dream*, 5.1.421-426, ed. Robert Arwan, Paul Bertram, and Jon Roberts (New York: Quality Paperback Book Club, 1997).

Fear not! The following is not a padded bibliography. Even professors dread those. Some of the books I quoted earlier are *not* on this list, and some I did not quote *are* on this list. Choose what will most nourish you from this menu. Use the Bible to test everything in my book and these.

Corporate Prayer

Crawford, Dan R. *Giving Ourselves to Prayer: An Acts 6:4 Primer for Ministry*. Terre Haute: Prayer Shop, 2008. Crawford has compiled 80 short pieces on prayer by a wide array of writers from different (even conflicting) orientations. The third section of the book has 20 pieces on corporate prayer.

Gundersen, David. A *Praying Church: The Neglected Blessing of Corporate Prayer*. Sand Springs: Grace & Truth, 2018. The first half teaches about prayer, and the second half provides 30 days of brief devotions about prayer that people can use in prayer meetings.

Head, David. *He Sent Leanness: A Book of Prayers for the Natural Man*. New York: Macmillan, 1959. This is the only tongue-in-cheek prayer book I have seen. He pokes redemptive fun at the church by forming prayers that reflect our foibles and failures.

Henderson, Daniel and Margaret Saylar. *Fresh Encounters: Experiencing Transformation Through United Worship-Based Prayer*. Carol Stream: NavPress, 2008. The authors work with a broader definition of corporate prayer than mine, but I resonate with their plea for the primacy of prayer as exemplified in Acts 2, with their diagnosis of cultural pathology, and with their call for pastoral leadership.

Hill, Megan. *Praying Together: The Priority and Privilege of Prayer in our Homes, Communities, and Churches*. Wheaton: Crossway, 2016. This is a fine, approachable book on the principles and practice of corporate prayer.

Huffman, Walter C. *Prayer of the Faithful: Understanding and Creatively Leading Corporate Intercessory Prayer*. Minneapolis: Augsburg Fortress,1992. Huffman has provided a helpful overview of the practice of liturgical prayer in worship services.

Lawless, Charles E. Jr. *Serving Your Church in Prayer Ministry*. Grand Rapids: Zondervan, 2003. This compact book is full of biblical perspective and practical advice. It brings evangelism and mission to the fore.

Longenecker, Richard, ed. *Into God's Presence: Prayer in the New Testament.* Grand Rapids: Wm. Eerdmans, 2002. Articles by a dozen scholars cover the Old Testament and cultural backgrounds to Christian prayer and survey key passages from the Gospels through Revelation.

McGraw, Ryan. *How Do Preaching and Corporate Prayer Work Together?* Grand Rapids: Reformation Heritage, 2014. I wish everyone would read this 26-page pamphlet. Following its lead could change everything for the better.

McGraw, Ryan. *How Should We Pray at Prayer Meetings?* Grand Rapids: Reformation Heritage, 2017. Here is another pamphlet packed with practical advice.

Onwuchekwa, John. *Prayer: How Praying Together Shapes the Church.* Wheaton: Crossway, 2018. This short book delivers a lot of value.

Spurgeon, Charles. *C. H. Spurgeon Autobiography.* Carlisle: Banner of Truth Trust, 1973. Susannah Spurgeon and Joseph Harrald originally compiled this work. The second volume tells Spurgeon's story from 1860-1892 and includes the role corporate prayer played in the famed preacher's ministry.

Tautges, Paul. *Pray About Everything: Cultivating God-Dependency.* Wapwallopen: Shepherd Press, 2017. The first part of this book orients the church to corporate prayer. Part two builds on that foundation with brief meditations for prayer meetings.

Church Health

Crowe, Jaquelle. *This Changes Everything: How the Gospel Transforms the Teen Years.* Wheaton: Crossway, 2017. People of any age can benefit from this wonderful book, especially from its lessons about being a body united across age groups.

Cymbala, Jim. *Fresh Wind, Fresh Fire: What Happens When God's Spirit Invades the Hearts of His People.* Grand Rapids: Zondervan, 1997. Pastor Cymbala tells the story of the Brooklyn Tabernacle Church and the crucial part prayer played in its growth.

Dever, Mark and Jamie Dunlop. *The Compelling Community: Where God's Power Makes a Church Attractive.* Wheaton: Crossway, 2015. The authors make the case for being truly attractional through gospel community rather than by treating church like a commodity.

Ferguson, Sinclair. *The Grace of Repentance.* Wheaton: Crossway, 2010. This small, compelling book presents the simple solution to many of our deepest problems.

Guinness, Henry Grattan. *The Revival in Ireland: Letters from Ministers and Medical Men in Ulster on the Revival of Religion in the North of Ireland Addressed to the Rev. H. Grattan Guinness.* Lexington: ULAN Press, 2013. This collection of letters shows how prayer is both the prod and the product of true revival.

Hawkins, Greg, Cally Parkinson, and Eric Arnson. *Reveal: Where Are You?* South Barrington: Willow Creek Resources, 2007. The leadership of Willow Creek Church hired prime consultants to do a vast spiritual audit of their church. The results are eye-opening.

McCraken, Brett. *Uncomfortable: The Awkward and Essential Challenge of Christian Community*. Wheaton: Crossway, 2017. This book is a much-needed tonic for an evangelical culture driven by marketing models.

Rainer, Thom. *Autopsy of a Deceased Church: 12 Ways to Keep Yours Alive*. Nashville: B&H, 2014. An experienced church consultant reveals a dozen traits that dying churches have in common, and he points to practices that promote health.

Stetzer, Ed and Thom Rainer. *Transformational Church: Creating a New Scorecard for Congregations*. Nashville: B&H, 2010. The chapter "Prayerful Dependence" is especially helpful in this book about the foundations of discipleship.

Storms, Sam. *To the One Who Conquers: 50 Meditations on the Seven Letters of Revelation 2-3*. Wheaton: Crossway, 2008. The letters in Revelation 2-3 are the Lord's evaluation of church ministries. These devotionals help us use the Lord's letters as God-given assessment tools.

Thorpe, Sam. *No Other Foundation: An Exposition of Acts 2:42*. Dubuque: ECS Ministries, 2010. Thorpe's short book points us to this crucial text as a model for healthy ministry.

Wilson, Jared. *The Prodigal Church: A Gentle Manifesto Against the Status Quo*. Wheaton: Crossway, 2015. Wilson does a humble but penetrating job of questioning common operating assumptions, and he points in a biblically healthy direction.

Leadership

Armstrong, John H. ed. *Reforming Pastoral Ministry: Challenges for Postmodern Times.* Wheaton: Crossway, 2001. This collection of 14 essays by various authors has especially helpful chapters about courageous leadership, church growth, and prayer.

Bounds, Edward McKendree. *Preacher and Prayer.* Breinigsville: Kessinger, 2010. This book was published in 1907 and changed my life a century later. This amazing work roots all ministry in prayer.

Carlson, Kent, and Mike Leuken. *Renovation of the Church: What Happens When a Seeker Church Discovers Spiritual Formation.* Downers Grove: IVP, 2011. The price these leaders were willing to pay for healthy change is a fortifying example of shepherding by conviction.

Mohler, Albert. *The Conviction to Lead: 25 Leadership Principles for Leadership that Matters.* Bloomington: Bethany House, 2012. This book is nicely arranged into 25 short sections, making it handy for discussion in leadership team meetings. It will take the kind of leadership Mohler describes to make necessary changes in our churches.

Stone, Charles. *People Pleasing Pastors: Avoiding the Pitfalls of Approval-Motivated Leadership.* Downers Grove: IVP, 2014. Stone deals with a fundamental problem that undermines many pastors and lay leaders alike.

Tripp, Paul David. *Dangerous Calling: Confronting the Unique Challenges of Pastoral Ministry.* Wheaton: Crossway, 2012. Tripp surveys unhealthy actions and attitudes of a congregation and its leaders. He points the way forward by reliance on the sovereign Savior.

Wilson, Jared. *The Pastor's Justification: Applying the Work of Christ in Your Life and Ministry*. Wheaton: Crossway, 2013. Though written to pastors, this outstanding book helps anyone involved in church life and ministry. It roots our significance in the gospel, not in our achievements.

Church and Culture

Brownback, Paul. *Counterattack: Why Evangelicals are Losing the Culture War and How They Can Win*. Maitland: Xulon, 2016. This book calls us to engage harmful cultural forces through divine love.

Hine, Thomas. *I Want That! How We All Became Shoppers*. New York: HarperCollins, 2002. The author traces the rise of the consumer culture in this fascinating and entertaining book.

Jethani, Skye. *The Divine Commodity: Discovering a Faith Beyond Consumer Christianity*. Grand Rapids: Zondervan, 2009. This is a potent exposé of the danger in approaching a church as consumers and of leaders using a consumer model.

Vassar, J. R. *Glory Hunger: God, the Gospel, and Our Quest for Something More*. Wheaton: Crossway, 2015. This book helps us all fight the narcissism that gets in the way of healthy ministry.

Wax, Trevin K. *Eschatological Discipleship: Leading Christians to Understand Their Historical and Cultural Context*. Nashville: B&H, 2018). Wax provides a stimulating presentation of biblical discipleship and rival worldviews like consumerism.

Wells, David F. *God in the Whirlwind: How the Holy-Love of God Reorients Our World*._Wheaton: Crossway, 2014. This book distills decades of reflections by an outstanding scholar with a heart for the church and the lost. He addresses challenges like consumerism and individualism, and he calls us back to biblical basics.

Bible Interpretation

Allen, Curtis. *Education or Imitation? Bible Interpretation for Dummies Like You and Me*. Adelphi: Cruciform, 2012. This is a brief and beneficial introduction to Bible interpretation.

Bargerhuff, Eric J. *The Most Misused Verses in the Bible: Surprising Ways God's Word Is Misunderstood*. Bloomington: Bethany House, 2012. The author uses 17 passages to illustrate how to respect context and to make proper application of God's word.

Schultz, Richard L. *Out of Context: How to Avoid Misinterpreting the Bible*. Grand Rapids: Baker Book House, 2012. This book highlights the corporate nature of many Bible passages as it addresses common interpretation missteps.